The Best Book of:
dBASE II™/III™

by

Ken Knecht

Howard W. Sams & Co., Inc.
A Subsidiary of Macmillan, Inc.
4300 West 62nd Street, Indianapolis, Indiana 46268 U.S.A.

International Standard Book Number: 0-672-22349-X
Library of Congress Catalog Number: 84-52376

Edited by: Elizabeth Burdett and Linnea Dayton, *Microtrend, Inc.,* San Diego
Interior Book Design by Michael Kelly, *The Word Shop,* San Diego

Printed in the United States of America.

Contents

Trademarks

Introduction

The dBASE II program by Ashton-Tate provides a very effective way to manage information and to prepare it for presentation. Ashton-Tate also markets a special version of dBASE II for 16-bit computers — the IBM PC, for example — called dBASE III. The two dBASE programs are very similar, but dBASE III has some additional features and does a few things differently. This book discusses dBASE II first. The differences between dBASE II and dBASE III are covered in the last two chapters. Once you learn how dBASE II works, you'll have no problem learning to use dBASE III.

DATABASES AND DATABASE PROGRAMS

The dBASE II and dBASE III programs are relational database programs. You use a command language to make them work for you. So what does all that mean?

What Is a Database?

Data is information. The Latin word *data* is the plural of *datum*, which means one item of information. Today data also has a singular, collective meaning, as the word group does.

A *database* is a collection of related information. Information in a database is stored as files. A *file* is a subgroup within the database. Let's look at an example of a database outside the realm of computers. We could consider a collection of metropolitan telephone books to be a database. The Seattle telephone directory can be considered to be a file within that database.

A *record* is a grouping of tightly related pieces of information. In our example, one line in the Seattle telephone book — containing a name, an address, and a telephone number — would constitute a record. That name is always associated with that particular address and telephone number.

A *field* is a specific piece of data within a record. In our telephone book record example, the name, address, and telephone number would be the three fields of the record. Each record in a file can be considered to have all the fields defined for the file. In other words, some records in our phone book may be printed as name and telephone number only, with no printed address. But these records are considered to have the standard three fields, with the address field left blank.

What Is a Database Program?

A *database* program is software that stores data, retrieves it, changes it, and permits it to be deleted. Usually, many other features are included.

Generally, a database program displays the data in a computerized database in columns and rows. You can visualize the data as being stored in that manner. For example, let's consider a simple computerized database with two columns and five rows, like this one, a personal phone book:

NAME	PHONE NUMBER
Jones, John	782-1234
Smith, Mary	213-4567
Fire Department	543-1357
Ed's Garage	782-9987
Short, Yvonne	782-1122

Each row constitutes a record, and each column constitutes a field.

The columns in this small, computerized database are NAME and PHONE NUMBER. The rows are the actual names and phone numbers stored under these headings. The dBASE II program will permit up to 32 columns, with up to 254 characters in each column entry. The total number of characters in a row is limited to 1000. The number of rows may not exceed 65,535. As you can imagine, this is ample space for most purposes. And if you really need to, there are ways to exceed these limits.

Because dBASE II and dBASE III are *relational* database programs, you can retrieve your data entries using any criteria you desire. For example, you can retrieve all the phone numbers that begin with 782, or perhaps all the names that begin with a letter between M and Z. Of course, you can also retrieve any specific phone number by entering a name, or vice versa. As you can see, there are many ways you can organize the data in your database.

If you wish, you can later change your database to include additional columns, such as an address column, without losing the names and phone numbers you have already stored.

It is also possible to retrieve all the data from any column in alphabetical or numeric order. Thus you could retrieve your data in alphabetical order by name or numeric order by phone number. As shown in the example, the order the data is entered in doesn't matter.

As you can imagine, a program like this can be used to organize almost any collection of data. Some examples are general ledger, accounts payable, accounts receivable, payroll, inventory, mailing list, records of stamp or coin collections, household inventory, vehicle mileage and expense records, budget records, and check registers.

THE dBASE COMMAND LANGUAGE

The *command language* mentioned earlier permits the informed user to manipulate the information in the database by giving English-like commands. This method is used instead of requiring the user to work through a set of menus and answer a series of questions. Once you learn the language — and it is not difficult — you'll find it the most convenient way to work with a database.

However, it is easy to create a program that provides menus and asks for any information required, to make life simpler for an uninformed user. Thus, dBASE II makes it easy for any user, experienced or not, to work with a database.

Creating a program that uses menus and questions is not very difficult, but it is time-consuming and requires testing to be sure everything works as intended. Several companies provide software that can write such programs automatically after being provided with a minimum of information. One such program is Quickcode by Fox and Geller. A little work with Quickcode will give you a dBASE II program that anyone can use. The same dBASE II enhancement could take several hours to write and test without Quickcode. If you wish to include features in your program that Quickcode doesn't supply, it's a simple matter to add them to the program yourself. Quickcode is discussed in Chapters 9 and 10.

Another program discussed in this book is dGRAPH, also by Fox and Geller. This program lets you use the data in your database to create many types of graphs. The dGRAPH program is described in Chapter 11.

Chapter 1

_____Getting Started_____

The dBASE II program can be run on computers that use or can accommodate the CP/M, MS-DOS, or PC-DOS disk operating system. This description is of version 2.4 of dBASE II.

The examples in this book were all tested on the IBM PC. There are only a few slight differences between using the program under CP/M and using it under MS-DOS (PC-DOS); these differences are mentioned at the appropriate points in the book.

To use the program on an IBM or similar machine, your system should meet the following requirements:

- An 8088-based microcomputer system
- 128K bytes of memory (minimum)
- MS-DOS or PC-DOS (disk operating system)
- One or more disk drives
- A cursor-addressable 80-column by 24-line CRT display (needed with full-screen operations)
- A text printer (optional)

All the examples in this book have been tested on an IBM PC with PC-DOS 2.0 192K bytes of memory, the IBM monochrome monitor, two 360K-byte floppy disk drives, a Davong 10 megabyte hard disk, and an Epson FX-80 printer.

Many other similar computer systems could be used. A list of the possibilities includes the Columbia 1600, Compaq, Cromemco 3102, Eagle 1600, Heath 89, IBM XT, IBM Display Writer, NEC APC, and TI Professional.

The requirements for a CP/M system include:

- An 8080-, 8085-, or Z-80-based microcomputer system (including Apple with a Z-80 card)
- 48K bytes of memory (minimum)
- One or more disk drives
- A cursor-addressable CRT (needed for full-screen operations)
- A text printer (optional)

Suitable computers include the Apple II+ with a Z-80 card, TRS-80 Model II, Northstar, and many others. A typical system might include an Apple II+ with an Apple III monitor, three Apple floppy disk drives, a Micro Pro CP/M card and operating system, a Videx 80-column card, and an Epson FX-80 printer.

Of course, it would be best to check out the suitability of your system with your dealer before you buy the program. Be sure you get the proper version of dBASE II for your system. The program must be furnished on a correctly formatted diskette for use on your specific system.

PROGRAM SPECIFICATIONS

Whatever system you are using, the program specifications for dBASE II are as shown in Table 1-1. Some of the numbers in the table may not mean much to you now, but most will be explained later.

Table 1-1. Program specifications for dBASE II

Characteristic	Capacity
Records per database file	65,535 (maximum)
Characters per record	1,000 (maximum)
Fields per record	32 (maximum)
Characters per field	254 (maximum)
Largest number	$+1.8 \times 10^{63}$
Smallest number	$+1 \times 10^{-63}$
Numeric accuracy	10 digits
Character string length	254 characters (maximum)
Command line length	254 characters (maximum)
Report header length	254 characters (maximum)
Index key length	100 characters (maximum)
Expressions in SUM command	5 (maximum)

Note that it would take a very, very large amount of disk space to make use of the largest possible file; that is, 65,535 records of 1,000 characters each for a total of over 65 megabytes. You probably won't be using files that large. However, you can see that dBASE II can fill up a floppy disk in a hurry, if you let it — especially an 18-sector, 35-track, single-sided floppy (about 160K bytes). Therefore, you'll find that in most cases the diskette capacity is the factor that limits the size of a database file. If this is a problem, you can break a too-large file down into several smaller ones (for example, a file for each month rather than one for the full year) or add a hard disk to your system. You can get hard disks with very large capacities, 20 megabytes or more. If you're still having space problems, your database might be better managed by a minicomputer or a mainframe. However, if you plan ahead, you should not be handicapped by your system's space limitations.

The numeric accuracy of dBASE II is 10 digits, which accommodates dollar figures up to $99,999,999.99. Using larger figures can lead to rounding errors.

BACKUPS

Before you start using your new dBASE program, be sure to make at least two copies of the master program diskette; then store the original master diskette in a safe place away from the copies.

As you are using the program, be sure to make copies of the diskettes containing your database files, too. This can be a nuisance, especially if you are using a hard disk, but you will consider the time well spent if you ever need to resort to using the backup. Re-creating a database from the printouts or other documents, or worse yet, from your own memory, can ruin your whole day — or week! It takes only one speck of dust, or a fingerprint, in a critical place to make a diskette unusable.

Floppy diskettes are very fragile and can easily be damaged by careless handling. Store them upright in dust-free containers and keep them away from heat and electric or magnetic fields. Equipment that can generate fields damaging to diskettes includes x-ray machines, vacuum cleaners, telephones, electric pencil sharpeners, printers, monitors, speakers, and even magnetized paper clips, or a carpet that generates static electricity. Anything that includes a motor or a magnet is dangerous and can destroy the data on your diskette. Also, don't write on a diskette or leave it lying around without its protective envelope. You can't be too careful!

PROGRAM INSTALLATION

After making backup copies of your dBASE diskette, the next step is to use one of your copies to install the program on your system. This relatively simple procedure is described in detail in your dBASE manual, so there's no need to repeat the directions here.

Once you have the computer's attention — usually indicated by the A> prompt from the disk operating system — type

INSTALL

(Your prompt might be a little different, depending on your system.)

You'll next be presented with a menu. Select your computer system from the list. If your computer system isn't on the list, consult the dBASE manual. You may need some help installing dBASE on a system that isn't listed. Try consulting your dealer if you can't get the program to work or if you don't understand the instructions in the dBASE manual.

If you are using CP/M, the INSTALL program asks several other questions. Refer to the dBASE manual. If you are in doubt about this answer, answer Y for the question about full-screen operations, press the RETURN key in response to the macro question, and see how things work out. If they don't, you can always run INSTALL again after you find out what the correct responses are.

FUNCTION KEYS AND COLOR

Your function keys can be programmed with your favorite dBASE II commands. The syntax goes something like this:

SET F1 TO 'HELP;'

or

SET F3 TO 'DISPLAY RECORD'

The single quotes must be included. If you program the F1 key as shown in the first example, pressing F1 will enter HELP followed by a carriage return (the ";" after HELP indicates the carriage return). If you use the syntax in the second example, pressing the F3 key activates DISPLAY RECORD. This command expects a number after it, so no carriage return is used.

If you don't change them, the function keys are set by the program as shown in Table 1-2. The book will not refer to the default functions by key, as these keys are not provided on all the computers that can run dBASE II. Also, if you do have the keys on your system, you might very well have changed them to other commands you prefer.

For computers that can display color, the SET COLOR command can be used. The syntax is

SET COLOR TO n1, n2

Table 1-2. Default function key settings for dBASE II

Key	Setting
F1	'HELP;'
F2	'DISPLAY;'
F3	'LIST;'
F4	'LIST FILES;'
F5	'LIST STRU;'
F6	'LIST STAT;'
F7	'LIST MEMO;'
F8	'CREATE;'
F9	'APPEND;'
F10	'EDIT *;'

where n1 is the color used for dim or reverse video display and n2 is the color for normal display. Possible values for n1 and n2 are as shown in Table 1-3.

Table 1-3. Display color settings

Setting	Display	
	Color CRT	Black and white CRT
0	Black	Black
1	Blue	Underline
2	Green	
3	Cyan	
4	Red	
5	Magenta	
6	Yellow	
7	White	
112	Reversed black on white	Reversed black on white

Unless you choose to change it, the program starts out with

SET COLOR TO 112, 7

Chapter 2

_____Creating a Simple Database_____

You have already run the INSTALL program. If you are just turning the computer on, use your DOS diskette to start up PC-DOS. Be sure to answer the date question when DOS begins. This date will be used by the program. Now, put your _copy_ of the dBASE II disk in drive A and type in dBASE in response to the A> prompt.

You'll get the dBASE II sign-on message, followed by a period at the beginning of the next line. This period is the dBASE II prompt; it indicates that the program is waiting for you to tell it to do something.

If you're using CP/M, you'll be asked for the date now. Use slashes, commas, or spaces between the month, day, and year. For example, January 2, 1984, could be entered 01/02/84, or perhaps 1,2,84, or even 01 2 84.

_____CREATING A DATABASE_____

Logically enough, the command used to create a database is CREATE. To get started, type in

    create

Now we have to decide what information we will be storing in our new database and what filename we will give it.

For the sake of example, let's make believe that we are the director of a zoo and need an inventory of the animals we have. First, we need a filename that gives a hint as to the content of the database. The filename may be up to eight characters long. It can include letters and numbers, and it must begin with a letter. In this case, how about ZOO? Enter ZOO in response to the dBASE II request to ENTER FILENAME:. Note that our responses to dBASE II requests can be in either uppercase or lowercase.

RECORD STRUCTURE

Now dBASE II wants to know what kind of information we are going to store in our database. As you can see by the prompt lines, dBASE II is looking for information about the fields: name, type, width, and number of decimal places.

The field name can be up to 10 characters containing only letters, digits, and colons. If colons are used, they must be embedded in the name; that is, the colon cannot begin or end the name. Note that no spaces or punctuation other than colons can be used. If the name you enter is not valid, dBASE II will tell you so.

It's a good idea to restrict your field names to nine or fewer characters. The reason for this will be explained when variables are discussed in the next chapter.

The field type can be character (C), numeric (N), or logical (L). A *numeric type* can contain digits only, with an optional single decimal point. The *logical type* field can contain either Y (yes) or N (no). The *character type* can contain letters, numbers, or punctuation marks.

The *width* is the maximum number of characters in the data we will be entering under that field name. If the type is logical, the length will be 1. If it's numeric, don't forget to count the decimal point, if any, in the width count. The maximum width is 254.

If the field type is numeric, and you will be using a decimal point, the number of decimal places you specify should be the maximum number of digits to *follow* the decimal point.

When making the entries to characterize the field, put commas, but no spaces, between the parameters, or information groups — NAME, TYPE, WIDTH, and DECIMAL PLACES. The computer supplies the field number. To signal the end of the entries for a field, press the RETURN key (<RETURN>) after the field number.

Here's how we'll enter the information for our inventory. From now on, the information the computer displays will be shown in uppercase, the user response in lowercase. This should make it easier to see who is saying what to whom. Remember, you can use uppercase for entries if you wish.

We have already typed in CREATE. Here are the prompts and some responses for our example:

ENTER FILENAME: zoo

ENTER RECORD STRUCTURE AS FOLLOWS:

NAME, TYPE, WIDTH, DECIMAL

FIELD	PLACES
001	animal,c,20 <RETURN>
002	quantity,n,3 <RETURN>
003	date,c,8 <RETURN>
004	:cage,n,3 <RETURN>

BAD NAME FIELD

004	cage#,n,3 <RETURN>

BAD NAME FIELD

004	cage no,n,3 <RETURN>

BAD NAME FIELD

004	cage:no,n,3 <RETURN>
005	sex,c,1 <RETURN>
006	value,n,7,2 <RETURN>
007	<RETURN>

The listing indicates that we had some problems with field number 004. First the name began with a colon — no good. The colon must be embedded. Then a # symbol was used — not allowed. The next try contained a space — not authorized. The final compromise used a colon to replace the space.

The <RETURN> directly after the field number 007 shows the use of the RETURN key to end the field entry sequence. From now on, field entry sequences will not include the instruction to press the RETURN key at the end of each entry. You must press the key, however, to indicate the end of each entry. You can have up to 32 fields.

Be very careful to enter all the fields in the example correctly. They can be changed after they are entered, but the method required for changing won't be discussed until Chapter 4, so try not to make any mistakes just yet.

If you do have to make corrections, you can start over from the beginning. Type

. delete file zoo

and press <RETURN>. Then enter all the fields again, starting with the create command, as shown on p. 19.

After you've finished entering the field information and pressed <RETURN>, you'll be asked if you want to enter any data now. Of course you do! So answer Y.

ENTERING DATA

You should next see a display consisting of your field names followed by one or more spaces, a colon, a line of some number of inverse blanks, depending on the width you selected, and another colon. You enter your data after each field name, ending with a <RETURN> if the full width of the line has not been used. Note that the display you see might be different than what's shown here if you are not using an IBM PC and a monochrome monitor. Later you'll find out how to change this display if you wish.

Since, if you're using CP/M you selected the full-screen editing mode during the installation of dBASE II, you have a lot of freedom when entering the data. You have the option of using the full-screen editing commands shown in Table 2-1. The ^ character indicates you should hold down the control (Ctrl) key while pressing the letter key.

Table 2-1.   dBASE II full-screen editing commands

Command	Function
^X	Moves the cursor to the next field
^F	Same as ^X
^E	Moves the cursor to the previous field
^A	Same as ^E
^D	Moves the cursor to the right
^S	Moves the cursor to the left
^V	Toggles between insert and overwrite modes
^G	Deletes the character under the cursor
^Q	Returns to the dBASE II command mode

You might find it easier to use the arrow keys in the keypad to move the cursor. If you're a WordStar user, you'll note that the control keys in dBASE II work much the same way. If you're using an IBM PC or XT, you can also use the left arrow key (backspace) in the top row of keys to back up. If not, you may or may not have a keypad, and your backspace key may or may not be in the top row.

If you try to move the cursor where it shouldn't be, you will be returned to dBASE II's command mode, the period prompt. In this case, just enter

. append

to get the next record number (or the number of the one you made the mistake in if you hadn't yet entered any data in the fields). Later in this chapter, you'll find out how to correct or delete any records you may have fouled up.

Now go ahead and enter the following animals into the database:

RECORD	ANIMAL	QUANTITY	DATE	CAGE	SEX	VALUE
00001	elephant	1	11/15/82	3	f	1000.00
00002	tarantula	1	11/12/83	15	m	5.00
00003	lion	2	02/05/80	1	m	101.00
00004	tiger	1	03/15/84	2	f	201.00
00005	lion	1	01/30/79	4	f	100.00
00006	tiger	2	07/04/81	5	m	200.00
00007	bear	3	02/05/83	11	f	150.00
00008	gorilla	1	06/12/80	9	f	2000.00
00009	python	1	09/27/76	14	m	175.00
00010	ant	2	01/12/84	10	f	0.03

Notice how, when you fill a field with its maximum number of characters, you get a beep and the cursor automatically moves to the next field. If you back up and type over an entry in a field, you can use the space bar to delete any characters left over from the old entry. If you enter too many digits after the decimal point, the extras will be deleted in the record. Note that they will be *deleted*, not rounded up.

Don't worry if you make a mistake on any of the records; you'll find out how to correct them soon.

Before we move on, you should know how to use the QUIT command if you wish to end a dBASE session and retain the data you've entered. First type ^W, and then

. quit

In case you haven't the time to complete this chapter at one sitting, be sure to use QUIT; don't just turn off the computer.

USE

We use the USE command to tell dBASE II what file we wish to work on. We can use this command at any point in the process of working with dBASE II. Opening a file with USE closes any file previously in use. The USE command without a filename closes any open file.

When you return to the program, type

. use zoo

to tell dBASE II which database to use. You can also employ the USE command to change to another database at any time.

LOOKING AT THE DATABASE

The LIST, LIST STRUCTURE, and DISPLAY commands let you view the database you've set up.

LIST

Now that you have entered all the records, use a ^Q to finish and return to the period prompt. To see what you have entered, type in

. use zoo

. list

You should see:

00001	elephant	1	11/15/82	3	f	1000.00
00002	tarantula	1	11/12/83	15	m	5.00
00003	lion	2	02/05/80	1	m	101.00
00004	tiger	1	03/15/84	2	f	201.00
00005	lion	1	01/30/79	4	f	100.00
00006	tiger	2	07/04/81	5	m	200.00
00007	bear	3	02/05/83	11	f	150.00
00008	gorilla	1	06/12/80	9	f	2000.00
00009	python	1	09/27/76	14	m	175.00
00010	ant	2	01/12/84	10	f	0.03

When you use LIST, dBASE II assumes you know what each field is the field names are not indicated.

LIST STRUCTURE

If you wish to review the details of the structure of your records, use

. list structure

This will give you all the details, thus:

STRUCTURE OF FILE: A:ZOO   .DBF

NUMBER OF RECORDS: 00010

DATE OF LAST UPDATE: 02/01/84 **(your date will be different)**

PRIMARY USE DATABASE

FLD	NAME	TYPE	WIDTH	DEC
001	ANIMAL	C	020	
002	QUANTITY	N	003	
003	DATE	C	008	
004	CAGE:NO	N	003	
005	SEX	C	001	
006	VALUE	N	007	002
** TOTAL **			00042	

Most of the information is self-explanatory. Note that the DATE OF LAST UPDATE: is the date you entered when you started up (booted) the computer. That's why it was important to use the correct date at that time. TOTAL is the record size. The maximum is 1000. The A: in front of the filename (ZOO) indicates the drive the file is stored on. The .DBF after the filename is dBASE II's way of indicating a database file.

Selective Listing

As mentioned earlier, if you use

. list animal, sex

you'll get a listing containing only the record numbers and the animal and sex fields. And

. list animal

will give you just the record numbers and animal fields. To omit the record numbers use

. list animal off

or

. list animal,sex off

The OFF command will work on all the LIST command variations. Now try

. list for animal = 'lion'

You'll see only records 3 and 5. Alternatively, you could use

. list for quantity>1

which would give you all the records that contain a quantity greater than 1. Using

. list for animal>'m'

will give you all the records whose animal field begins with a character later in the alphabet than "m" (records 2, 4, 6, and 9). Entering

. list animal,quantity for animal>'m'

shows you records 2, 4, 6, and 9, but only the animal and quantity fields.

Relational operators are symbols used to indicate a comparison between two values. The relational operators used in dBASE are shown in Table 2-2.

Remember to surround any compared character or characters with single or double quotation marks. Using the single quote (apostrophe) doesn't require the use of the Shift key. If you enter your data in uppercase, you might prefer to use the double quote (").

If you have more records than will fit on the screen, you can use ^S to stop and start the scrolling of the listing.

You should experiment with these relational commands until you understand them well. They are one of the most useful types of commands you can use when searching a large database.

As mentioned earlier,

. list structure

Table 2-2.   dBASE relational operators

Operator	Function
<	Less than
>	Greater than
=	Equal to
>=	Greater than or equal to
<=	Less than or equal to

shows you the record structure.
You can use

    . list files

to see the names of all the database files (.DBF) on the drive you are using. To see the names of files on another drive, use the LIST command as follows:

    . list files on b

displays the names of files on drive B, for example. Note that there is no colon (:) following the drive letter. You can also use an asterisk as a wildcard to display some of the files on a particular drive, but not others: The * wildcard stands for "any filename." For example, use

    . list files like *.com on b

to see all the files with the .COM suffix on drive B.
You can use the standard DOS wildcard file commands also. For example,

    . list files like d*.*

will list all the files beginning with the letter "D." And

    . list files like d????.*

will list any file with a five-letter name beginning with "D."

DISPLAY

You can use DISPLAY almost anywhere you've been using LIST and get the same results, except that

. display all

rather than

. display

accomplishes the same function as

. list

The DISPLAY command will show up to 15 records at a time; pressing any key will advance you to the next 15. You can type

. display record 4

or

. 4

. display

to see record 4.

Using

. display

by itself shows you the last selected record. If you have not yet selected any records,

. display

will show you record 1. If you then enter

. display next 4

you'll see records 1 through 4. (Not very logical; you'd expect to see 2 through 5, but that's the way it works.)

If it's easier for you to remember, you can use

. goto 4

. display

or

. go 4

. display

to view record 4. Then a

. skip 3

RECORD :00007

. display

will show you record 7. At this point,

. skip -5

RECORD :00002

. display

will provide you with record 2.
Entering the commands

. go top

. display

will display record 1, and

. go bottom

. display

gets you the last record (record 10 in our example).

ADDING RECORDS

Two commands, APPEND and INSERT, allow you to add records to the database.

APPEND

You have already learned one way to add records. Simply type

. append

to add a record or records to the list. If you had just started dBASE II or had been using another file, you would use

. use zoo

. append

to tell the computer you wanted to add another animal to the zoo database.

INSERT

Earlier you were told you could add records to the database with the APPEND command. However, APPEND always adds the new record to the end of the database list. If you wish to add a record to the beginning or middle of the list, you'll need to use the INSERT command. Thus

. 4

. insert before

will insert the new record before record 4. You enter the data the same way you do with APPEND. You will now have a new record 4, the old record 4 will now be record 5, and so on.

INSERT lets you enter only a single record, unlike APPEND, which will let you go on entering records forever (65,535 times is almost forever).

BROWSE and EDIT

The BROWSE and EDIT commands allow you to view and change database records.

BROWSE

The BROWSE command can be used to look at your records or to edit them. You have a choice of the fields to display; you don't have to look at all of them. To look at the animal and cage:no fields only, for example, enter

. browse fields animal,cage:no

Entering

. use zoo

. browse

will display all the fields. BROWSE shows you up to 19 records on the screen at one time. The display in response to

. use zoo

. browse

looks like this:

RECORD # :00001

ANIMAL---------------	QUA	DATE----	CAG	S	VALUE--
elephant	1	11/15/82	3	f	1000.00
tarantula	1	11/12/83	15	m	5.00
lion	2	02/05/80	1	m	101.00
tiger	1	03/15/84	2	f	201.00
lion	1	01/30/79	4	f	100.00
tiger	2	07/04/81	5	m	200.00
bear	3	02/05/83	11	f	150.00
gorilla	1	06/12/80	9	f	2000.00
python	1	09/27/76	14	m	175.00
ant	2	01/12/84	10	f	0.03

Note that the field names have either been extended with dashes or truncated (cut off short) to match the field width.

To move around in the file, you can use the control keys described earlier. To make moving easier, use the arrow keys if you have them. The left and right arrows move the cursor a single space in the direction indicated. The up and down arrows move the cursor from field to field. PgUp moves the display up one record; PgDn moves it down one record. When you are moving around in the file, the selected record's number will be shown after RECORD # in the first line. Also, the selected record will be displayed as inverse text (black characters on a white background).

If you wish to edit, you can simply type over the characters you want to change; a space deletes the character you type over. The cursor position shows you which character and field will be affected. The RETURN key will store the data in that field; an arrow key will let you leave the field. Note that you must select another record (inverse text) to make the change permanent. If you make a change in a record, then type ^Q with that record still selected, the change you made will be lost.

However, using a ^W accomplishes the QUIT action of ^Q but enters the record change, even if the record remains selected.

Using BROWSE in this manner is the easiest way to make changes in your records. BROWSE is, of course, also useful if you wish to do just that — browse through the records to see what's there.

When using BROWSE, if the fields widths total more than 80 characters, you can use ^B to move the rest of the fields into view, ^Z to move back again.

EDIT

Another way to edit is to use

. edit

The following prompt will appear:

ENTER RECORD # :

You should respond with either a record number or <RETURN> to get back to the command mode. Let's enter 10. The computer responds with

```
RECORD #  00010
ANIMAL    : ant
QUANTITY :  2:
DATE      :01/12/84:
CAGE:NO   : 10:
SEX       :f:
VALUE     :  0.03:
```

The data is displayed in inverse video. The cursor indicates the field and character position. You can use the control keys or the arrow keys to move from field to field and within the fields. As in the BROWSE mode, you must leave the record, or use ^W, to make any changes permanent. To leave the record, you can use the down arrow key to move past the last field, or use PgDn. The ^W command leaves the record and returns to the RECORD # prompt with any changes intact. If you use ^Q, you'll be returned to the RECORD # prompt but you'll lose your changes. If you use the down arrow or PgDn key, you'll be asked for another record number to edit. Pressing <RETURN> will get you back to command mode.

You can also specify the record you want to edit as follows:

. edit 10

In this case, when you leave the record you'll get the period prompt. You could use

. edit 8,10

to edit records 8 through 10. As you finish each record, you'll be presented with the next in the series you specified. Either ^Q or ^W will get you back to the period prompt before the series is completed.

If you use

. edit 11

dBASE II will tell you

RECORD OUT OF RANGE

(there are only 10 records) and will give you the period prompt. However, if you tell it

. edit 8,11

you'll get records 8 through 10 and no error message. If you change record 8, then use PgDn to get to record 9, and then use ^Q, the change in record 8 will be retained.

If you use

. edit 8

then when you use PgDn to leave the record, you'll get record 9, then 10, then the period prompt. You can leave with the ^Q or ^W.

If you use

. edit

ENTER RECORD # :

and respond with an 8, PgDn will get you record 9, then record 10, then another

ENTER RECORD # :

So you see, EDIT can be useful for changing records, but BROWSE may be easier to use.

DELETING AND RECALLING RECORDS

Records may be deleted, and deleted records may then be reinstated.

DELETE

To delete a record, use ^U in BROWSE or EDIT, with the record selected. As long as you remain in BROWSE or EDIT, using ^U on a deleted record will bring the record back again.

When you use LIST, a deleted record is shown with an asterisk (*) in front of the first field. In EDIT mode, you'll see DELETED on the first line, after the record number. If you edit a deleted record, your change will be made, but the record will remain deleted.

You can also delete a record by using

. delete record 4

The following will appear:

00001 DELETION(S)

You can get the record back with

. recall record 4

00001 RECALL(S)

Other possibilities for deleting are

. delete all for quantity >1

00004 DELETION(S)

and

. delete next 4

Be careful with these. Obviously, they make it easy to delete the wrong records. Another command to be careful with is

. delete zoo

This one gets rid of the whole file. And the dBASE program gives you no way to get it back! Be careful.

RECALL

If you use

. delete all for sex = 'f'
00003 DELETION(S)

you can use

. recall all for sex = 'f'
00006 RECALL(S)

to get the records back (if you haven't used PACK, discussed on page 37). (We got the extra RECALLS because of the earlier DELETE ALL FOR QUANTITY>1.)
Now use

. recall all

to return the zoo database to normal.

ERASE

ERASE is the command that clears the screen. ERASE has no effect on your database. Thus

. erase

results in the period prompt at the top of a blank screen.

CALCULATOR MODE

If you need to do a little calculating, use this mode. The command is the question mark. You could also consider the ? to mean "WHAT IS?". Thus

. ? 2 + 2

results in

4

If you ask

. ? 7/3

the result will be

2

but you get the following results if you include decimal places:

. ? 7.0/3
2.3
. ? 7.000/3
2.333
. ? 7/3.0
2.3

If you ask

. ? 2+4*5

you will get

22

but

. ? (2+4)*5

gives

30

Get the idea? The ? can also be used to obtain nonnumeric data. And also,

. 4
. ? animal
tiger
. 10
. ? animal
ant
. ? sex
f

PACK

Until now, any deleted records could be undeleted with a ^U in BROWSE or EDIT mode. They were marked as deleted but remained in the database. To delete records permanently and remove them from the listings or displays, use the PACK command. If you inserted a record at position 4 when you tried the INSERT command, delete that inserted record. You should then have 11 records, with only record 4 marked as deleted. Now use PACK and LIST:

. pack

PACK COMPLETE, 00010 RECORDS COPIED

. list

You'll get back only the original 10 records.

Be careful; once you use PACK, deleted records are gone forever. You can no longer use ^U to undelete them.

HELP

You can get some help concerning the syntax and use of the various commands by typing HELP followed by the command you are interested in. For example,

. help display

will show you information about the DISPLAY command, if your version of dBASE II includes the HELP feature.

Chapter 3

_____More About dBASE II Data_____

Our next step in learning to use dBASE II is to examine the types of data we're storing and determine how we can manipulate it.

_____CONSTANTS_____

A _constant_ is a data item (value) that remains the same; that is, it is not changed to something else by the program or the operator. In dBASE II terminology, a constant can be set to a numeric value, a logical value, or a character string. A constant is also referred to as a _literal value_ — it means what it says; it does not refer to some other value.

A _numeric value_ is a number, with or without a decimal point. Examples of numeric values are 1, 5.5, 1000, and so on.

A _logical value_ is a value for TRUE or FALSE. A logical value for TRUE can be T, t, Y, or y; the value for FALSE, F, f, N, or n. You must use one of these single letters. Of course, the N stands for no, the Y for yes.

A _character string_ is a group of one or more characters. It is also possible to have a _null string_, one containing no characters. The characters may be enclosed in single quotes (apostrophes), double quotes, or square brackets. These are called _delimiters_. Thus, you can have 'STRING' or "STRING" or [STRING]. Note, however, if you use one of these delimiter characters within a string, you must use different delimiters to enclose the string. Thus, some examples of acceptable strings are

'A [is an angle bracket.'

and

"Enter the user's last name."

But you can't use

'Enter the user's last name.'

because you can't enclose a single quote (apostrophe) within single-quote delimiters. That makes sense. If you do, when dBASE II sees the apostrophe in user's, it will assume the apostrophe is the closing delimiter; then it will have no idea of what to do with the remainder of the string.

You can put numbers within delimiters. If you do so, they are no longer considered numeric values and they cannot be used in calculations. Thus "3" is a string, not a numeric constant.

Referring back to the last chapter, you'll recall that the command "?" could be translated as "what is?" Thus,

. use zoo

. ? animal

would produce the response,

elephant

You get "elephant" because when you first open the file, the USE command assumes that you want record 1. The creature in the animal field in record 1 is an elephant. However, if you enter

. ? 'animal'

you'll get

animal

because placing the string *animal* in delimiters causes dBASE to see it as a constant (or literal), not the name of the animal field. What you ask for is what you get!

If you'll refer back to Chapter 2, you'll see that you were using constants when you used the LIST command. For example,

. list for animal = 'lion'

In this case, 'lion' is a character string constant. You used a numeric constant when you entered

. list for quantity $>$ 1

The 1 was a numeric constant. See how it works?

VARIABLES

Variables in dBASE II are of two types; one type is the *record field name*, the other is the *memory variable*.

We encountered the record field name variable when we set up the ZOO database. Some of the record field names we used were animal, cage:no, sex, and so on. We saw that, for example, animal could be used to represent an elephant, a lion, a tiger, and an ant, among others. To see what variable animal represents in a record, we need only point at that record and type

. ? animal

Animal can represent any data in the animal field of any record.

MEMORY VARIABLES

The other type of variable (the memory variable) can be used to represent any value — logical, string, or numeric; it does not have to be data in one of the records. Memory variables will be explained further in the discussion of the STORE statement, later in this chapter.

We can have up to 64 memory variables in use at any time. If we need more, we can save some or all of the first 64 in a disk file, and then use the variables we saved to store new information. We can rename these reused variables too.

Memory variables can be very handy to store a value temporarily.

The construction of a memory variable name follows the same rules as for a record field name; that is, it must begin with a letter and consist of letters, numerals, or embedded colons, with no spaces or other punctuation. The maximum length is ten characters.

STORE

As you will see later on, you will frequently wish to temporarily store the contents of a record field variable — animal, for example — in a memory variable. To make the variable easy to recognize, it is usual to place the prefix "M" before the field variable to create the memory variable; this makes it obvious what is stored in the memory variable. For example,

. 4

. store animal to manimal

tiger

. ? manimal

tiger

We'll see more examples of the use of memory variables when dBASE II programs are discussed later in the book. Using field names of nine or fewer characters, as suggested in Chapter 2, allows you to add the "M" prefix without exceeding the 10-character limit.

In the above example, *manimal* is a character variable, because the data stored in it is in character form. This is an example of storing the contents of one variable, animal, in another, manimal. We can also store a character constant in a variable.

. store 'ROBERT' to name
ROBERT

or

. store 'this is a message' to message
this is a message

You can store up to 254 characters in each of the 64 memory variables, but the total number of characters stored in all 64 variables cannot exceed 1536 (an average of 24 in each variable).

We can also store numeric or logical data in a memory variable.

. store 3 to three
3
. store 6 to six
6

The type of data stored in a variable is remembered and stored with the variable. If we use

. store '12' to twelve
12

we have made twelve a character variable that stores the string '12'. Because we can do arithmetic with numeric variables, but not character or logical variables, we can't do arithmetic with the variable twelve.

Note that "three," "six," and "twelve" would generally be very poor choices for variable names; they were used only to make their contents easy to remember when they appear in examples later.

We can change the data stored in a variable at any time. Of course, we will then lose what was stored in the variable before we made the change.

```
. store 24 to number
24
. ? number
        24
. store 48 to number
48
. ? number
        48
```

We can also change the type of data stored in a variable.

```
. store 'something' to mixed:up
something
. ? mixed:up
something
. store 100 to mixed:up
100
. ? mixed:up
        100
. store T to mixed:up
.T.
. ? mixed:up
.T.
```

The last data stored to mixed:up was the logical value T. This is not a string (notice that it has no delimiters). Instead, it has meaning to dBASE II. The ".T." syntax used in the display indicates that it is a logical variable.

Anytime we wish, we can see what is stored in the variables. To see all of them, try

. display memory

MANIMAL	(C)	tiger
NAME	(C)	ROBERT
MESSAGE	(C)	this is a message
THREE	(N)	3
SIX	(N)	6
TWELVE	(C)	12
NUMBER	(N)	48
MIXED:UP	(L)	.T.

TOTAL 08 variables used   00072 BYTES USED

You could also use

. list memory

to get the same result.

You can do arithmetic with the numeric variables.

. ? six/three

    2

. ? six — three

    3

. store six/three to two

2

. ? two

    2

. ? six + 8

    14

But look what happens if you try

. ? twelve

12

. ? twelve/six

*** SYNTAX ERROR ***

Remember, twelve stored the string constant '12' and is a character variable, not a numeric variable.

RELEASE

To erase a variable and thereby free up one of those 64 valuable memory variables, use

. release message

to delete the memory variable message. Don't do it yet, but if you use

. release all

you'll erase all the memory variables, both names and contents. Try deleting a few variables, one at a time, followed by

. display memory

to see the effect after each RELEASE. Finally, use

. release all

and try displaying the memory variables again. As you'll see, they're all gone now.
Another variation of RELEASE is

. release all like m*

which would release all the variables that begin with the letter M. The asterisk (*) represents any remaining characters. If you used

. release all like A?C

you'd release any variables containing three letters, no more and no less, with A the first, C the third, and any character in the second position.

In the opposite manner,

. release all except A?C

would do just as it says.

Obviously, you have to be careful with wildcard commands like these, or you could end up losing the wrong variables. And once they're gone, you can't get them back.

OPERATORS

Operators are symbols or words that are used in expressions. dBASE has four kinds of operators — arithmetic, relational, logical, and string operators.

Arithmetic Operators

You are probably familiar with the dBASE *arithmetic operators* as shown in Table 3-1.

Table 3-1.   Arithmetic operators

Symbol	Function
( )	Grouping
*	Multiplication
/	Division
+	Addition
–	Subtraction

Parentheses are used to group operations. Operations within parentheses are performed before those outside parentheses. You can put parentheses within parentheses; this is called *nesting*.

In arithmetic operations, there is an order of precedence of operation; that is, some operations are always performed before others. The order is first multiplication and division, then addition and subtraction. (You can use the phrase "My Dear Aunt Sally" as a memory aid.) Outside this order, operations are performed from left to right. Here are a few examples.

. ? 2 + 4 − 3

3

The operations were addition and subtraction, so there was no precedence. The operations were performed from left to right.

    . ? 2 + 4 * 6
       26

The multiplication was performed first, then the addition.

    . ? (2 + 4) * 6
       36

The addition was in parentheses so it was performed before the multiplication.

    . ? 3 * 16 / 2 + 2
       26

The multiplication and division were performed first, from left to right, then the addition.

    . ? 16 / 2 * 3 + 2
       26

Same result, different order (division, multiplication, then addition).

    . ? 16 / 2 * (3 + 2)
       40

The addition was done first because it is in parentheses, then the division (left to right), then the multiplication.

    . ? 16 / (2 * 3 + 2)
       2

First the multiplication within parentheses, then the addition within parentheses, then the division.

If the standard order of operations is not correct for the result you desire, use parentheses to force the order you wish. Try a few examples of your own.

Relational Operators

Relational operators are used to perform comparisons between different variables or between variables and constants. Table 3-2 lists these operators.

Table 3-2. Relational operators

Symbol	Function
=	Equal to
<>	Not equal to
>	Greater than
<	Less than
>=	Greater than or equal to
<=	Less than or equal to

Relational operators were used in the preceding chapter in the discussions of LIST and DELETE.

Logical Operators

Logical operators are used to perform several comparisons within the same command line. Logical operators are listed in Table 3-3.

Table 3-3. Logical operators

Symbol	Function
.NOT.	Inverts the logic (true becomes false, and vice versa)
.AND.	Requires that both parts of a comparison be true
.OR.	Requires only that either of two parts of a comparison be true

Note that parentheses can be used with logical operators. There is no established precedence, so you might have to use parentheses to ensure the precedence you desire.

Let's look at some examples of the use of logical operators.

. use zoo

. list for animal > 'g' .and. quantity = 1

You should get records 2, 4, 5, and 9. Now try

. list for (quantity = 1 .AND. sex = 'f') .OR.
value = 150

You should get records 1, 4, 5, 7, and 8. Notice the parentheses. Try leaving them out to see the difference.

The relational and logical operators are what make dBASE II such a powerful program. Try some examples of your own to understand how they work. Be sure to use the periods before and after NOT, AND, and OR. If you don't, you'll get a syntax error. Also, be careful of a command such as

. list for quantity >= 1 .OR. sex = 'm'

This quantity comparison will select everything.

String Operators

As the name implies, *string operators* are used for character strings (variables or constants). Table 3-4 shows the string operators used by dBASE.

Table 3-4.   String operators

Symbol	Function
$	Indicates a substring
+	Concatenation; doesn't remove trailing spaces
−	Concatenation; removes trailing spaces

The *substring* command looks to see if the string variable or constant before the dollar sign is contained in the string following the dollar sign. The string following the dollar sign can be a string variable or a string constant. Note — any variables used must be string variables, not numeric variables.

. list for '80' $ date

This will list records 3 and 8, records in which the date contains the string '80'. Note that

. list for 80 $ date

will get you a syntax error for your trouble. It won't work because 80 is a numeric constant, not a string constant.

To separate records containing the month of 01 from those containing a day of 01, you'd have to get pretty complicated. To get a list of dates with the month 01, you could use

. list for ('01' $ date .AND. .NOT. '/01' $ date)
  .AND. '01/01' $ date

This assumes that the month and day are separated with a backslash (/). The last .AND. '01/01' was needed to get the date of 01/01/??, which would otherwise have been rejected by the first expression (the expression in parentheses). When functions are discussed in Chapter 7, we'll see a much easier way to handle this.

When you wish to join two strings together, you use *concatenation*. Here's an example.

. ? 'TO' + 'GET' + 'HER'

TOGETHER

As you can see, the + operator is used to join two or more strings together. This is what the $5.00 word "concatenation" means.

Remember that a string shorter than the field length was padded with blanks (spaces). For example, the field length for animal was set at 20, and therefore, elephant is stored as elephant plus 12 trailing spaces. So if you say

. 1

. ? animal + ", " + sex

you get

ELEPHANT   , F

But if you say

. ? animal − ", " − sex

you get

ELEPHANT,F

In the second example, the 12 blanks after elephant were moved to the end of the displayed line, where they are not visible. If the − operator is used for concatenation instead of the +, any trailing blanks following the string in a variable are moved to the end of the displayed line. Because you will generally have trailing blanks whenever record field variables are used, you'll normally want to use the − concatenation operator.

Another way to eliminate any trailing spaces is to use the TRIM function. This will be discussed in the "Functions" section in Chapter 7.

Be sure to experiment with the operators presented in this chapter before you move on; they are very important!

Chapter 4

Dealing with the
Entire Database

This chapter introduces you to some very useful commands that work on an entire data file, rather than specific records.

COPY

You'll use COPY to reproduce a database under another filename, usually temporarily. You'll see an example of reproducing a database to a temporary file in the "Sorting and Indexing" section of this chapter.

To COPY the entire ZOO database, including ZOO's structure (see Chapter 2), to another file — let's call it TEMP (for temporary) — use

. use zoo

. copy to temp

00010 RECORDS COPIED

. use temp

You now have an exact copy of the ZOO database in the file TEMP. You can use LIST or DISPLAY STRUCTURE to verify this.

Whenever you use COPY, the file copied to (in this case, TEMP) if it already exists, is destroyed. So watch those filenames for duplication.

51

To COPY only the structure of a database, you'd use

. use zoo

. copy to temp structure

. use temp

This time you'll have only the structure of the ZOO file stored in TEMP, which you can verify by typing

. display structure

There it is! If you type

. list

you'll verify that the data was not copied along with the structure, as it was in the first example. Copying a file structure has its uses, as you'll soon see.

Finally, you can COPY only part of the structure, by naming the fields you wish to copy with

. use zoo

. copy to temp structure fields animal,cage:no,sex

. use temp

You'll see only the animal, cage:no, and sex fields when you use

. display structure

As before,

. list

will show that the data itself has not been transferred. Later you'll see how to use APPEND to move data to the selected fields.

Now we'll see some uses for COPY.

SORTING AND INDEXING

The order in which you enter data may not necessarily be the best order for displaying it. Later, when printing reports, you will probably wish to reorganize the data in some manner. Usually this means arranging the records by ordering the entries in one of the fields in numeric or alphabetical order. You have two choices if you wish to order the data in a field in this manner: to sort it or to index it. Sorting is easy, so let's start with that method.

SORT

When you *sort*, you permanently rearrange the records in the file, in the order you request, by field name. You can sort on any of the fields, in ascending or descending order. You can also sort on more than one field.

First, let's sort the ZOO file using the animal field. To do this, use

. use zoo

. sort on animal to temp

SORT COMPLETE

. use temp

You can't sort a file to itself; that is,

. sort on animal to zoo

is *not* allowed. You're probably beginning to see one use for COPY. You can, for example, sort the zoo file on *animal* and store the result in TEMP; then COPY TEMP to ZOO after sorting. As with COPY, if the TEMP file you sort to already exists, it will be destroyed and replaced by the new data and structure.

You can now use

. display structure

to see that ZOO and TEMP both have the same structure. But now use

. list

00001	ant	2	01/12/84	10	f	0.03
00002	bear	3	02/05/83	11	f	150.00
00003	elephant	1	11/15/82	3	f	1000.00
00004	gorilla	1	06/12/80	9	f	2000.00
00005	lion	2	02/05/80	1	m	101.00
00006	lion	1	01/30/79	4	f	100.00

00007	python	1	09/27/76	14	m	175.00
00008	tarantula	1	11/12/83	15	m	5.00
00009	tiger	1	03/15/84	2	f	201.00
00010	tiger	2	07/04/81	5	m	200.00

You'll see that the sort has organized all the animals in alphabetical order. The SORT command uses ascending order as its default, and the animal field was sorted because that's what we requested. (A *default* is the condition or value dBASE II chooses when you do not specify a choice.) Obviously, all the other data for each animal (sex, cage:no, etc.), moved along with the animal name.

Note that when character data is sorted alphabetically, it is sorted in ASCII order. That means that uppercase letters come before lowercase letters. Thus, LION comes before Lion or ant. This is one of the few instances in which the case of the characters means anything. To get consistent sorting, be sure all your data is either in uppercase or lowercase.

To digress for a moment, ASCII stands for American Standard Code for Information Interchange. Each character is represented by a number between 0 and 255, which is called its ASCII value (sometimes, redundantly, ASCII code). Each is stored in one byte in the computer's memory. This system is used by almost all computers and software. When data is sorted, smaller ASCII values are placed before larger ones. ASCII values for the uppercase letters run from 65 through 90, lowercase from 97 through 122, and the digits from 48 through 57.

To get the sorted data in TEMP back into the ZOO file, simply use

. copy to zoo

00010 RECORDS COPIED

. use zoo

As mentioned earlier, it is possible to sort on more than one field.

. use zoo

. sort on value to temp ascending

SORT COMPLETE

. use temp

. copy to zoo

00010 RECORDS COPIED

. use zoo

. sort on animal to temp

SORT COMPLETE

. use temp

. copy to zoo

00010 RECORDS COPIED

. use zoo

. list

00001	ant	2	01/12/84	10	f	0.03
00002	bear	3	02/05/83	11	f	150.00
00003	elephant	1	11/15/82	3	f	1000.00
00004	gorilla	1	06/12/80	9	f	2000.00
00005	lion	1	01/30/79	4	f	100.00
00006	lion	2	02/05/80	1	m	101.00
00007	python	1	09/27/76	14	m	175.00
00008	tarantula	1	11/12/83	15	m	5.00
00009	tiger	2	07/04/81	5	m	200.00
00010	tiger	1	03/15/84	2	f	201.00

When you do this, sort on the least important field first, then the next least important, and so on. You can do this for as many fields as you wish.

If you're the cautious type, a firm believer in Murphy's Law, then before sorting, copy the original unsorted file to another file for safekeeping in case something goes wrong during the sorting operation. Remember, however, that this will mean having three copies of the file in existence most of the time, and if the file is a long one, you may not have room on the disk for all three copies.

As you can see, sorting is easy. However, in a large database, sorting is slow. Also, you'll have to sort again, probably, when you add new data to your database. You could use the INSERT command (Chapter 2) to enter the new data in alphabetical order, but there's an easier way.

INDEXING

Indexing is much faster than sorting, and added items can be automatically inserted in the correct order. Also, in an indexed database, a specific record can be found by field item very quickly (two seconds or less), if you have indexed that field.

To ensure that your database is the same as the one used here, check yours against the order shown in the listing in the "Sorting" section. If yours differs from this order, correct it now.

Since the ZOO file is already sorted by animal field, we'll index using another field. Try

. use zoo

. index on cage:no to cages

00010 RECORDS INDEXED

. use zoo index cages

. list

00005	lion	2	02/05/80	1	m	101.00
00009	tiger	1	03/15/84	2	f	201.00
00003	elephant	1	11/15/82	3	f	1000.00
00006	lion	1	01/30/79	4	f	100.00
00010	tiger	2	07/04/81	5	m	200.00
00004	gorilla	1	06/12/80	9	f	2000.00
00001	ant	2	01/12/84	10	f	0.03
00002	bear	3	02/05/83	11	f	150.00
00007	python	1	09/27/76	14	m	175.00
00008	tarantula	1	11/12/83	15	m	5.00

You should see your ZOO file listed in cage-number order. Just what did we do? The

. use zoo

command, of course, made sure we were using the correct file. The

. index on cage:no to cages

created a sorted index file. The index file (cages) contains a list of all the record numbers in order by cage number. The command

. use zoo index cages

tells dBASE II to use the cage number order when listing the zoo file. Note, you don't use the command

. use cages

because cages is an index file, not a database file.

You can see the result of

. use zoo index cages

if you type

. list

Note that the original ZOO file is untouched and is still in animal-sorted order as we left it. When you index a field in a file, there is no danger of damaging the original file. Other advantages of indexing are that only one copy of the file, the ZOO file, remains on the disk; the index file is a much smaller file, as it contains only one field and the record numbers; and an index file can be created much more quickly than a file can be sorted.

If you wish to index a numeric field, you must use a function to convert the numeric field to a character field. Try this:

. use zoo

. index on str(value,7,2) to cost

00010 RECORDS INDEXED

. use zoo index cost

. list

00001	ant	2	01/12/84	10	f	0.03
00008	tarantula	1	11/12/83	15	m	5.00
00005	lion	1	01/30/79	4	f	100.00
00006	lion	2	02/05/80	1	m	101.00
00002	bear	3	02/05/83	11	f	150.00
00007	python	1	09/27/76	14	m	175.00
00009	tiger	2	07/04/81	5	m	200.00
00010	tiger	1	03/15/84	2	f	201.00
00003	elephant	1	11/15/82	3	f	1000.00
00004	gorilla	1	06/12/80	9	f	2000.00

Note the 7,2 following value in the INDEX statement. This is the same 7,2 you used when you created the file and established the value field back in Chapter 2. It means the field is seven characters wide and there are two decimal places. This specification is required to put blanks in front of the numbers as necessary, so they will sort correctly by ASCII code. For example "55" will come before "6", but " 6" (notice the space in front of the 6) will come before "55." A space has a lower ASCII value (32) than a digit.

You can index as many fields in a file as you wish. However, using more than one index will tend to slow things down, because all the indexes are updated after alterations of the database. It's best to have only one index file for a database. Then it can be automatically updated when it is included in the USE command.

To get around this limitation, you can put several fields in one index file. Try this:

. index on animal + str(value,7,2) to anival

00010 RECORDS INDEXED

Note that the index file is not *animal*, but *anival*, short for *animal value*.

Unlike what happens with a sorted file, when you include the index file in a USE command, and then use APPEND, EDIT, REPLACE, PACK, and so on, the changes are reflected in the index file in use.

When an index file is included in a USE command, positioning commands such as GO, GO BOTTOM, SKIP, GO TOP, and so on, operate in relation to the indexed order.

As mentioned earlier, if several index files are used with a file, it will take longer for the computer to make changes. But if you wish to use this feature, use this new command

. set index to cost,cages,anival

where COST, CAGES, and ANIVAL are index file names. (You can read more about this new command in Chapter 7.) Then do the EDIT, APPEND, REPLACE, or other command. Use

. set index to

without index filenames to release the index(es) previously set.

So that we will be working with the same index files and database, make sure you have created all the index files previously discussed; that is, CAGES, COST, and ANIVAL.

REINDEX

If for some reason you think an index file has been messed up, perhaps by the use of an APPEND command when the USE command didn't specify an index file, you can easily re-create the index files. The command

. reindex

will rebuild any index files mentioned in a USE or SET INDEX TO command. The program tells you which indexes have been reindexed as they are completed.

DISPLAY STATUS

DISPLAY STATUS will tell you the status of the database file in use. DISPLAY STATUS allows you to look at a file's structure and at all the items within the file. That way you can review before you enter a command that will make changes in the file.

. use zoo index cost

. display status

DATABASE SELECTED — A: ZOO   .DBF

PRIMARY USE DATABASE

INDEXES: KEY EXPRESSION:

A: COST   .NDX   str(value,7,2)

TODAYS DATE   — 05/05/84

DEFAULT DISK DRIVE   — A:

ALTERNATE	— OFF	BELL	— ON
CARRY	— OFF	COLON	— ON
CONFIRM	— OFF	CONSOLE	— ON
DEBUG	— OFF	DELETE	— OFF
ECHO	— OFF	EJECT	— ON
ESCAPE	— ON	EXACT	— OFF
INTENSITY	— ON	LINKAGE	— OFF
PRINT	— OFF	RAW	— OFF
STEP	— OFF	TALK	— ON

FUNCTION KEY ASSIGNMENTS

KEY	ASSIGNMENTS
F1	HELP;
F2	DISP;
F3	LIST;

F4	LIST FILES;
F5	LIST STRY;
F6	LIST STATUS;
F7	LIST MEMO;
F8	CREATE;
F9	APPEND;
F10	EDIT #;

SEARCHING THE DATABASE

FIND

To use FIND, you must include an index file in the USE command. FIND uses the selected indexed field data to find any record. For example,

. use zoo index cages

. find 15

. display

will find the record that has 15 in the cage:no field. This would be record 8, the tarantula. You can also use a partial name. For example,

. use zoo index anival

. find py

. display

will find record 7, the python, even though the ANIVAL index record for the python is "python   175.00." The FIND command will find the first-used index record that matches the data given, even if the whole field is not matched.

If no match is discovered, FIND will return a message:

. find XX

NO FIND

You can also FIND memory variables. To demonstrate this, first create the memory variable to be found. Use the STORE command to creat the memory variable, as discussed in Chapter 2:

. go 1

. store animal to manimal

ant

Then use FIND:

. find &manimal

. display

This will find record 1, the ant. Note that the ampersand (&) is used before the memory variable name.

Note that delimiters are not required around the FIND data. You can use them if you wish, and they must be used if the data contains leading spaces. Remember, numeric labels in an index file may contain leading spaces.

If you use

. set exact on

before using FIND, only an exact match will be displayed. The string following the FIND command must exactly match all the characters in the index file entry (except for trailing blanks). To turn this off, you use

. set exact off

as you might have guessed.

FIND will retrieve deleted records. If you *don't* wish this to happen, use

. set delete on

To turn it off, use

. set delete off

If the record found is one of several that will match, you can use the LOCATE command (explained next) to find the others. For best results, try to make the data following FIND specific enough to pinpoint only the record you are after.

The main advantage of FIND is that it will find a record very quickly, usually within two seconds or less. The FIND command is one good reason to use an index file. Remember, FIND will work only on an index file mentioned in the USE command.

LOCATE

LOCATE works in much the same way as the LIST FOR command (Chapter 2), but displays only the record number of the located record(s), one at a time if it has found more than one. For example,

. use zoo

. locate for animal = 'e'

RECORD: 00003

. display animal

00003 elephant

Of course, you can use any DISPLAY command, or any other command, after the record number is given.

You can carry out a relational search.

. locate for animal> = 'p'

RECORD: 00007

. display animal

00007 python

. continue

RECORD: 00008

. display animal

00008 tarantula

. continue

RECORD 00009

. display animal

00009 tiger

. continue

RECORD: 00010

. display animal,cage:no

00010 tiger   5

. continue

END OF FILE ENCOUNTERED

As you can see, CONTINUE will continue searching for data matching that in the LOCATE command, until you tell it to quit or until the end of the file is reached. You can use more complicated commands such as

. locate for sex = 'f' .and. value>1000

RECORD: 00004

. display animal

00004 gorilla

Each new LOCATE command starts at the beginning and searches the entire database. LOCATE will work faster on a file that is USEd *without* an index file.

_____CHANGING THE FILE STRUCTURE_____

MODIFY

The MODIFY command is used if you wish to change your file structure, add a new field, change the size of a field, or perform a similar operation.
Warning: You can erase a database if you use this command incorrectly. Never, never use it on an original database — only on a copy!
Here's how to use MODIFY:

. use zoo

. copy to temp structure

. use temp

. modify structure

MODIFY ERASES ALL DATA RECORDS . . . PROCEED?   (Y/N)

y

	NAME	TYP	LEN	DEC	
FIELD 01	:ANIMAL	C	020	000	:
FIELD 02	:QUANTITY	N	003	000	:
FIELD 03	:DATE	C	008	000	:
FIELD 04	:CAGE:NO	N	003	000	:
FIELD 05	:SEX	C	001	000	:
FIELD 06	:VALUE	N	007	002	:

FIELD 07 :   :

FIELD 09 :   :

. . .

FIELD 22 :   :

You can now edit the record structure as you did with the BROWSE command (Chapter 2) to change it in any way you wish. You can change field names, add new fields, and so on. But be careful about changing field names or types, because your old data won't automatically be transferred to these new field names. Type in any new changes under the previous data.

When you've finished, you may wish to use

. display structure

to be sure you have it the way you want it. Now use

. append from zoo

00010 RECORDS ADDED

to move all the data from the old ZOO database into the new TEMP database. Only data under matching field names will be moved. Any new fields or changed fields will be left blank.

Now use

. list

to be sure all the appropriate data was transferred correctly.

You now have your new database and structure in TEMP. If you wish, and if you are certain you've done everything correctly, you can move the new data to ZOO. When you enter the following command, your original ZOO data and structure will be gone forever, so be sure that's what you want to happen.

. copy to zoo

00010 RECORDS COPIED

The old data and structure are replaced with the modified structure and appropriate data from TEMP.

To be sure the data was transferred properly, enter

. use zoo

. list

Then if you wish,

. delete file temp

to get rid of the no longer needed TEMP file.

Let's review the first few steps. Be sure to use the

. use zoo

. copy to temp

. use temp

steps *before* you use MODIFY. Of course, you can give the COPY command any filename that is not being used. It's a good idea to do a lot of double-checking, because MODIFY has much potential for disaster.

APPEND – An Alternative to MODIFY

We saw one example of using APPEND earlier, when we discussed MODIFY. Here's another APPEND example. Recall from the beginning of this chapter, that it is possible to copy only part of the structure. To repeat

. use zoo

. copy to temp structure fields animal,cage:no,sex

. use temp

Remember, this copied only the three named fields in the structure to TEMP; no data was transferred. To move the data, use

. append from zoo

00010 RECORDS ADDED

. list

00001	ant	10	f
00002	bear	11	f
00003	elephant	3	f
00004	gorilla	9	f
00005	lion	4	f
00006	lion	1	m
00007	python	14	m

00008	tarantula	15	m
00009	tiger	5	m
00010	tiger	2	f

You have now transferred all the data in the three named fields from ZOO to TEMP. This might be useful if you wished to get rid of some of the data fields that are no longer relevant to your database. This procedure is easier than using MODIFY.

CHANGING DATA

The REPLACE and CHANGE commands can be used to change data already entered into the database.

REPLACE

You can replace all the data in a field with some other data. For example, if you decide to increase the value of all the animals by 10 percent, you can do this:

. use zoo

. replace all value with value*1.1

00010 REPLACEMENTS

. list

00001	ant	2	01/12/84	10	f	0.03
00002	bear	3	02/05/83	11	f	165.00
00003	elephant	1	11/15/82	3	f	1100.00
00004	gorilla	1	06/12/80	9	f	2200.00
00005	lion	1	01/30/79	4	f	110.00
00006	lion	2	02/05/80	1	m	111.10
00007	python	1	09/27/76	14	m	192.50
00008	tarantula	1	11/12/83	15	m	5.50
00009	tiger	2	07/04/81	5	m	220.00
00010	tiger	1	03/15/84	2	f	221.10

You can replace any field with any type of data you wish. Of course, you can use arithmetic expressions only with a numeric field.

Notice the "all" that was included in the REPLACE command. If this were left out, only the current record would be acted upon.

Now use

. set index to anival,cost

. reindex

REINDEX   INDEX FILE   —   A: ANIVAL   .NDX

00010 RECORDS INDEXED

REINDEX   INDEX FILE   —   A: COST   .NDX

00010 RECORDS INDEXED

. set index to

to update the ANIVAL index and the COST index files, which, as you'll remember, includes the value field.

This next command statement is very complex. Don't run it on your ZOO file.

. replace all value with value*1.1,cage:no with

cage:no + 100 for quantity>1

If you'd like, run it on a copy of ZOO; that way, the ZOO database we're using won't get messed up.

At this point, check to ensure that your ZOO database looks like the one listed on p. 66 after the first REPLACE command.

. replace all value with value*1.1

CHANGE

This command lets you change any of the data in any of the fields, one field at a time. Let's say you want to change the quantity of pythons to 2. Do this:

. use zoo index anival

. find p

. change field quantity

RECORD: 00007

QUANTITY: 1

TO   2

You might prefer to use the EDIT command instead. Sometimes it's quicker. However, if you're changing several fields in several records, you would probably prefer CHANGE. In this case, you could use

. use zoo

. change all field quantity,animal for sex = 'f'

Here you'd be presented with the quantity and animal field contents for possible change in all records where the sex field contained an "f." The FOR is optional, and you can use one or more field names after FIELD. Not the ALL after CHANGE.

If a record field is blank, put a space after the CHANGE? question. To delete the data in a field, use Ctrl Y after the TO. To get out of a series of CHANGEs, use the Escape key.

Chapter 5

Creating Reports

Sometimes you will want your list of data to be printed in a special format. This is an easy operation with dBASE II's built-in REPORT command. You can also use REPORT for screen display.

You can tailor a report to almost any format you wish. You can include any or all the record fields and include totals of any of the numeric fields. You can use relational commands so that only selected records will be included in the report.

If you use

. set eject on

before the report is printed, a page will be ejected before any printing is done. To turn it off, use

. set eject off

as you might suspect.

REPORTS WITHOUT SUBTOTALS

Let's start by printing a sample report. Our example will show how the dialogue goes and what the results are. Then the answers will be explained.

. use zoo

. report

ENTER REPORT FORM NAME: costlist

ENTER OPTIONS, M = LEFT MARGIN, L = LINES/PAGE, W = PAGE WIDTH:

m = 5,1 = 55,w = 80

PAGE HEADING? (Y/N) y

ENTER PAGE HEADING: Zoo Inventory

DOUBLE SPACE REPORT? (Y/N) n

ARE TOTALS REQUIRED? (Y/N) y

SUBTOTALS IN REPORT? (Y/N) n

COL   WIDTH,CONTENTS

001   20,animal

ENTER HEADING: Kind of Animal

002   6,quantity

ENTER HEADING: Stock

ARE TOTALS REQUIRED? (Y/N) y

003   4,sex

ENTER HEADING: Sex

004   11,value

ENTER HEADING: Value Each

ARE TOTALS REQUIRED? (Y/N) n

005   12,value*quantity

ENTER HEADING: Total Value

ARE TOTALS REQUIRED? (Y/N) y

006   <RETURN>

The report is then displayed on the screen so you can review it before printing. If you type

. report form costlist to print

you'll get the following print-out.

PAGE NUMBER. 00001

05/08/84

Zoo Inventory

Kind of Animal	Stock	Sex	Value Each	Total Value
ant	2	f	0.03	0.06
bear	3	f	165.00	495.00
elephant	1	f	1100.00	1100.00
gorilla	1	f	2200.00	2200.00
lion	1	f	111.10	111.10
lion	2	m	111.10	222.20
python	2	m	192.50	385.00
tarantula	1	m	5.50	5.50
tiger	2	m	221.10	442.20
tiger	1	f	221.10	221.10
** TOTAL **				
	16			5182.16

If you use

. report form costlist to print for sex = 'f'

you will get the following result:

PAGE NUMBER. 00001

05/08/84

Zoo Inventory

Kind of Animal	Stock	Sex	Value Each	Total Value
ant	2	f	0.03	0.06
bear	3	f	165.00	495.00

elephant	1	f	1100.00	1100.00
gorilla	1	f	2200.00	2200.00
lion	1	f	111.10	111.10
tiger	1	f	221.10	221.10
** TOTAL **				
	9			4127.26

Next time you use this report form name (COSTLIST), you won't have to answer the questions again, because dBASE II will have saved your answers in the file COSTLIST.FRM. You'll have to delete this file

. delete file costlist.frm

FILE HAS BEEN DELETED

if you want to change the format of the report while still using that same report name. This report form name is a filename and must follow the filename conventions mentioned early in the book.

If you don't specify options for the left margin width (M), the number of lines printed on each page (L), and the width of the page (W), the defaults used by dBASE II are M = 8, L = 57, and W = 80. The W option is used only to center the report heading.

The PAGE HEADING is the report name.

The DOUBLE SPACE REPORT? prompt does just that if you answer with a Y.

The ARE TOTALS REQUIRED? question permits you to total selected numeric data columns if you wish.

The SUBTOTALS IN REPORT? prompt supplies subtotals if answered affirmatively. An example will be given later in the chapter.

COL is the column number in the report and is supplied by the program. WIDTH is the width of that report column; this need not be the width entered in the file structure, but it should generally be at least as large as that width. If it isn't that wide, the program will print data in a column on more than one line if necessary.

CONTENTS means the contents of that column in the report. It can be a field name or an expression. The expression can contain any combination of record field names, constants, and memory variables. If you concatenate a ' . . . ' to the contents (for example, animal + ' . . . '), the dots will be added to the contents. We'll see a demonstration of this in the next example, a subtotal report. If the contents become too large to fit within the column width, they will be printed on more than one line; the line will be broken at a space, if possible. This lets you squeeze more data into a report if you run out of page width.

The HEADING is the name printed above the column in the report. If the heading is too long for the column width, it will be printed on more than one line.

In this case, keep the word length to the column width or less to avoid split words. Column headings are normally centered. Entering a < at the left of a column heading will left justify it; a > will right justify it.

The ARE TOTALS REQUIRED? question is asked for each column of numeric data if you answered this question affirmatively when it was asked at the beginning of the report. If you answer Y, the total is printed at the bottom of that column.

To finish the report format, use the RETURN key to answer the COL number prompt, as shown for column 6 of the example.

If you wish to use an additional heading on a single report, you can use, for example,

. set heading to SPECIAL REPORT

Of course, this must be used before the report is printed. Set it before you use the REPORT command. You can also use

. set date to 5/8/84

if you want a date other than the system date to appear on the report.

The two report lines in the examples show a few of the available options. First,

. report form costlist to print

uses the COSTLIST.FRM file (the one you filled out), and sends the result to the printer. If you left off TO PRINT, the report would be displayed on the screen. The next example illustrates the use of relational commands. The other line,

. report form costlist to print for sex = 'f'

uses the same report format but prints only those records for which the sex field is "f." You can use .AND., .OR., and .NOT. to expand this FOR option (with parentheses as required). Examples of this use of .AND. and .OR. were given in earlier chapters, in the discussion of the LOCATE command in Chapter 4, for instance.

REPORTS WITH SUBTOTALS

. use zoo

. set eject off

. set date to 5/8/84

. set heading to SPECIAL REPORT BY SEX

. report

ENTER REPORT FORM NAME: bysex

ENTER OPTIONS, M = LEFT MARGIN, L = LINES/PAGE, W = PAGE WIDTH: <RETURN>

PAGE HEADING? (Y/N) y

ENTER PAGE HEADING: Animals by Sex

DOUBLE SPACE REPORT? (Y/N) n

ARE TOTALS REQUIRED? (Y/N) y

SUBTOTALS IN REPORT? (Y/N) y

ENTER SUBTOTALS FIELD: sex

SUMMARY REPORT ONLY? (Y/N) n

EJECT PAGE AFTER SUBTOTALS? (Y/N) n

ENTER SUBTOTALS HEADING: Animal Sex

COL   WIDTH,CONTENTS

001   23,animal + ' . . . '

ENTER HEADING: <Animal

002   5, quantity

ENTER HEADING: In Stock

ARE TOTALS REQUIRED? (Y/N) y

003   <RETURN>

Now, we'll print the report on the screen:

. report form bysex to print

PAGE NO. 00001   SPECIAL REPORT BY SEX

05/08/84

                              Animals by Sex

Animal   In
                              Stock

* Animal Sex f

ant   . . .   2

bear	. . .	3
elephant	. . .	1
gorilla	. . .	1
** SUBTOTAL **		
		7

* Animal Sex m

lion	. . .	2
** SUBTOTAL **		
		2

* Animal Sex f

lion	. . .	1
** SUBTOTAL **		
		1

* Animal Sex m

python	. . .	2
tarantula	. . .	1
** SUBTOTAL **		
		3

* Animal Sex f

tiger	. . .	1
** SUBTOTAL **		
		1

* Animal Sex m

tiger	. . .	2
** SUBTOTAL **		
		2

** TOTAL**

16

Hmm! Not so good. It seems that the program doesn't collect all the records into the proper group before it subtotals. It just takes them as they come. So let's do this:

. index on sex to sex

00010 RECORDS INDEXED

. use zoo index sex

. report form bysex to print

PAGE NO. 00001   SPECIAL REPORT BY SEX

05/08/84

                              Animals by Sex

Animal		In Stock
* Animal Sex f		
ant	. . .	2
bear	. . .	3
elephant	. . .	1
gorilla	. . .	1
lion	. . .	1
tiger	. . .	1
** SUBTOTAL **		
		9
* Animal Sex m		
lion	. . .	2
python	. . .	2
tarantula	. . .	1
tiger	. . .	2
** SUBTOTAL **		
		7
** TOTAL **		
		16

Ah, that's more like it.

Here is an explanation for the material that was added when we returned a Y in response to the SUBTOTALS IN REPORT? question.

The ENTER SUBTOTALS FIELD: prompt wants to know what criteria to use to divide the report into subtotals. In this case, the sex field was used. Since there are two possible contents in the sex field, F and M, the program printed two subtotal reports (after it was properly indexed by sex). The name selected must be a record field name. If, for example, the ANIMAL field was selected, then there would have been eight subtotal reports, one for each different animal (if the file was indexed or sorted on the animal field).

If you answered Y to the SUMMARY REPORT ONLY? you'd get only the subtotals for each subtotal report. Try it.

The EJECT PAGE AFTER SUBTOTALS? prompt, if answered in the affirmative, would start a new page for each subtotal report.

Finally, the ENTER SUBTOTAL HEADING: prompt wants to know what you wish to print at the beginning of each subtotal group.

More examples of reports will be given when we create some command files later on.

COUNTS AND TOTALS

dBASE provides several ways of keeping track of counts and computing totals for reports.

COUNT

The COUNT command can be useful in reports. It lets you count the number of occurrences of something in your database. The results can be sent to a memory variable.

```
. use zoo

. count all for sex = 'f'

COUNT  =  00006
```

There are six animal entries whose sex is female.

```
. count all for sex = 'f' .and. quantity>1

COUNT  =  00002
```

There are two female animal entries with more than one animal.

. count for animal>'e'

COUNT = 00007

There are seven animal entries starting with letters later in the alphabet than "e." Both of these two series of commands:

. count for animal>'e' to mcount

COUNT = 00007

. ? mcount

7

and

. count to mcount for animal>'e'

COUNT = 00007

. ? mcount

7

store a count in a memory variable. The command series

. go 1

. count next 5 for sex = 'f'

COUNT = 00004

starts with the first record and counts the number of female entries in the first five entries. COUNT ALL and COUNT perform the same function

. count all

COUNT = 00010

. count

COUNT = 00010

SUM

To get a total of a numeric column of a selected group of records for a report, use SUM.

. use zoo

. sum quantity * value to mtotal

5182.16

. ? mtotal

5182.16

The total value of all the animals is $5182.16. This total has been stored as a memory variable.

. sum quantity * value for sex = 'f' to cost

4127.26

. ? cost

4127.26

The total value of all female animals is $4127.26. The total has been stored in the variable "cost."

. sum quantity for sex = 'f' .or. (sex = 'm' .and.

value>150)

13

There are 13 animals that are either female or have a value greater than $150.

. sum quantity,quantity * value

16 5182.16

There are 16 animals altogether, and they have a total value of $5182.16. Using SUM is a good way to get numeric summaries out of a database very quickly and conveniently.

TOTAL

TOTAL works like the SUBTOTALS option in the REPORT command but sends the extracted data to another file instead of printing or displaying it.

The database you are getting the data from must be indexed on the field you are using in the command, as was the case for REPORT SUBTOTALS. Unless you index to group the animals, each record will have its own total.

First, let's set up a TEMP file to use in our example.

. use zoo

. delete file temp

FILE HAS BEEN DELETED

. copy to temp structure fields animal,quantity,value

Now,

. index on value to cost

00010 RECORDS INDEXED

. use zoo index cost

. total on value to temp

00008 RECORDS COPIED

. use temp

. list

00001	ant	2	0.03
00002	tarantula	1	5.50
00003	lion	3	222.20
00004	bear	3	165.00
00005	python	2	192.50
00006	tiger	3	442.20
00007	elephant	1	1100.00
00008	gorilla	1	2200.00

See what happened? This was not a very practical example, but it does illustrate how the command works. In categories with more than one listing (lion and tiger) the entries were consolidated without regard for sex, and the value entries were totaled. This would be more useful if you had, let's say, a list of part numbers and sales for each part by the day. To get the grand total of sales for each part, you would set up TEMP with the part number and sales fields. Index on the part number field in the original file. Total on sales to TEMP. It's done.

You'll see more examples of using the COUNT, SUM, and TOTAL commands later in the book.

Chapter 6

_____dBASE II Command Files_____

Wouldn't it be nice if anyone could use a database without knowing all those commands we've been studying in the first five chapters? Could add, delete, and change records and print reports just by answering a few questions or selecting choices from a menu? Well, that's what command files are for.

A _command file_ is simply a series of dBASE II commands. By themselves, the commands we have learned so far are not quite enough to do the job. But if we add a few more, we can make a command file that will do almost anything we wish. This chapter will discuss some of these additional commands and show some simple command files in use.

First of all, how do we create a command file?

. modify command test

Now you have a blank screen and can use the full-screen editing commands discussed in Chapter 2 to create the command file. Because we used TEST in the command line, the command file will be named TEST.PRG (TEST.CMD if you're using CP/M).

MODIFY COMMAND is the built-in editor. Start your editing near the beginning of a file and work toward the end.

Note: If you understand how to program in some other language, such as BASIC or Pascal, you'll see a lot of similarity between such a program and a dBASE II command file.

Now, let's write a simple command file using our old friend, the ZOO database file. Start with

. modify command test

Now enter the following commands:

. use zoo

. copy structure to temp fields animal,quantity,sex,value

. use temp

. append from zoo

. list for sex = 'f'

. count for sex = 'f' to sexcount

. display memory

. ? "isn't that marvelous!"

. ^w

The ^W command caused you to leave the editor and return to the dBASE II command mode. The file was also saved. Now type

. do test

and watch your file do its thing.

```
00010 RECORDS ADDED
00001      ant          2      f                    0.03
00002      bear         3      f                  165.00
00003      elephant     1      f                 1100.00
00004      gorilla      1      f                 2200.00
00006      lion         1      f                  111.10
00009      tiger        1      f                  221.10
COUNT  =  00006
SEXCOUNT   (N)   6
**TOTAL**  01 VARIABLES USED   00007 BYTES USED
isn't that marvelous!
```

Very nice, but rather useless. Hang in there, it gets better!

GETTING KEYBOARD INPUT

Three dBASE commands — INPUT, ACCEPT, and WAIT — provide ways to get input from the keyboard.

INPUT

To get a response from the keyboard while a command file is running, use this command. It will accept any data constant and will display a prompt if you want it to. Character data must be enclosed within delimiters. The data received will be stored in a memory variable you select. Remember, only 64 variables can be active at one time.

. input 'Quantity?' to mquant

Quantity? : 20

    20

The prompt, Quantity? in this case, is optional. The INPUT command would print the prompt on the screen, followed by a colon, and wait for a response, in this case a numeric constant. If the operator tried to enter a character string not enclosed in delimiters, a ** SYNTAX ERROR ** would result. The value entered would be stored in the memory variable MQUANT. (See Chapter 3 for a review of memory variables, if necessary.) The entry of the number must be terminated with the RETURN key.

You can use INPUT to get a logical response, too. For example

. input 'Finished?' to done

Finished? : t

.T.

This time the program is looking for a logical response: F, f, T, t, Y, y, N, or n. See Chapter 3 for a review of logical (Boolean) data. Of course there is no way you can guarantee that someone using the command file will make one of these single-letter responses, so there is always a possibility that your plans will go awry. The single letter does not need to be enclosed in delimiters, so long as it is a legal logical response character. A <RETURN> is necessary to complete the response.

The program can tell a logical response from a character response of a single letter matching the legal logical characters, because a character response has to be surrounded by delimiters, but a logical response does not.

As mentioned, you can use this INPUT command to prompt for a character string, too. But if you do, the operator will have to remember to use delimiters around the string — square brackets or single or double quotes. In real life, this is a lot to expect. So, if a character string is required, it's better to use the ACCEPT command.

ACCEPT

This command behaves the way INPUT does, but it works *only* for character strings. The operator's response does *not* have to be enclosed within delimiters.

. accept 'Last name?' to lname

Last name? : Jones

. ? lname

Jones

As written, this command sequence would store the character string entered from the keyboard, Jones, to the memory variable LNAME. The prompt is optional. The keyboard input must be terminated with <RETURN>. Thus for ease of use, it is best to use INPUT for numeric or logical responses and ACCEPT for character strings. This makes it consistent for the operator.

WAIT

The WAIT command provides another way to get input from the keyboard. WAIT will accept a *single* character from the keyboard, and the use of the RETURN key to complete the entry is *not* required (or desired).

Using WAIT can cause confusion. Once operators learn to use the RETURN key after every entry, they get confused (and logically so) when WAIT is used and the RETURN key is not required. They will usually use the RETURN key anyway, and the <RETURN> then takes the place of the next requested entry, completely fouling everything up! Be consistent; the operator will appreciate it.

If you decide to use WAIT, this is how you do it:

. wait

WAITING

By itself, this command will cause the program to move to the next command when any single key is pressed. The value of the key pressed is not stored. If you use

. wait to mrecall

WAITING y

. ? mrecall

y

the value of the key pressed is stored in the memory variable MRECALL. Note that no prompt can be used in the WAIT command.

We'll cover one good use for WAIT next.

DISPLAYING DATA
_____AND ERASING THE SCREEN_____

The ? Command

You can use the ? command discussed in Chapter 2 to display data. Remember, the ? can be followed by a constant, a field or memory variable, or an expression. If the ? is used alone, the display will skip a line, which is sometimes helpful. The ? and WAIT combination can also be helpful:

. ? 'Press the RETURN key to continue'

. wait

This saves wasting a memory variable in this situation.

ERASE

The ERASE command will clear the screen. It also releases all outstanding GETs. (The GET command will be covered later in this chapter.)

SAY

SAY is a better way to place data on the screen or printer.

When you use ? to put something on the screen, it will be displayed on the following line in sequence. Often this is all right, but sometimes you will wish to put the data elsewhere on the screen; for example, you may be trying to reproduce a form familiar to the operator.

. erase

. @ 10,20 say 'Hello'

. @ 20,40 say 'Goodbye'

This will put Hello at row 11, column 21, and Goodbye at row 21, column 41. The preceding ERASE clears the screen.

Note: 0 is the number of the first row and column. Row 0, column 0 is the upper left corner of the screen. Row 23, column 79 is the lower right corner (on the IBM PC).

Avoid using row 0, as dBASE II uses it from time to time. (Recall that rows are the horizontal lines on the screen; columns are the vertical character positions in the rows.)

Depending on how you answered the questions when you installed your system (Chapter 1), you may see the characters following SAY displayed at half intensity or in reverse video.

If you use

. @ 20,0

without the SAY, then row 21 will be entirely erased. If you use

. @ 10,20

row 11 from column 21 to the right edge of the screen will be erased.

There is a command

. set format to screen

that should be used before a SAY command is used. When dBASE II starts up, this command is automatically set (it is the default). But it could be changed for printing as we'll see later. When in doubt about whether this command is still in effect, use it just in case before using SAY commands directed to the screen.

The prompt following SAY can be a string constant, as shown in the example. Or it can be a field or memory variable or an expression. Thus

. erase

. set format to screen

. store 10 to ten
        10

. store 5 to five
        5

. store 'testing' to test

testing

. store 'here' to here

here

. @ 12,5 say ten

. @ 14,5 say five

. @ 16,5 say five * ten

. @ 18,10 say test

. @ 20,10 say here

. @ 22,10 say test + ' ' + here

Note that the contents of the variables were repeated as they were stored. This also happens when INPUT or ACCEPT is used, as was noted when these were described. When we're entering data as we've been doing so far, that's all right. But in a command file, we don't want all that clutter to appear on the screen to confuse the operator. To avoid that, use

. set talk off

to keep such clutter off the screen. Then use

. set talk on

to bring things back to normal. To try this out, turn TALK off at the beginning of the last example list, and turn TALK back on after the last command. Note that setting TALK off does not affect the SAY commands.

Relative SAY

You can use relative coordinates with SAY commands. The $ represents the previous coordinate. Thus, for

. @ 5,1 say 'way'

. @ $ + 1,$ say 'over'

. @ $ + 3,$ + 40 say 'there'

the equivalent absolute SAY commands would be

. @ 5,1 say 'way'

. @ 6,1 say 'over'

. @ 9,41 say 'there'

Note that offsets for the printer can be positive only. Screen offsets may be negative.

GET

The GET command is used in conjunction with SAY to get a response from the operator. The GET command is followed by a field or memory variable name.

You can use GET only 64 times maximum; then you must use CLEAR GETS or ERASE to release the GETs. The CLEAR GETS command will not clear the screen as ERASE does. Usually ERASE is used to clear the screen in preparation both to accept more data and to release the GETs.

A memory variable must already exist in order to be used by a GET.

If a field variable is used, it must be a valid one for the file being USEd. When the SAY . . . GET command is displayed, any value in the field variable will be displayed as well. This is effective if you are using SAY . . . GET to edit an existing record. But if you are using SAY . . . GET to add a new record to the file, you should use

. append blank

before using SAY . . . GET. This will be illustrated shortly.

Note that when displaying with SAY on the screen, you can have the pairs of vertical and horizontal coordinates in any order. But when printing, you must put them in consecutive order, because the printer won't back up.

READ

Finally, to actually enter the data (or change the data) in the variable following the GETs, the READ statement is used. This causes the cursor to move to each field in turn. At each field you can enter some data followed by <RETURN>, or use the RETURN key alone to skip that field and move on to the next.

Before we create a command file to illustrate these commands, we'll need to know another new command.

DO WHILE

DO WHILE creates a loop and allows us to repeat a series of commands.

DO WHILE (some condition is true)

    statement 1

    statement 2

    . . .

    statement n

ENDDO

One of the statements following the DO WHILE is used to make the DO WHILE condition false and thus end the loop. Or a statement can escape the loop by jumping out of it.

You will find DO WHILE to be very useful in command files. Here's an example using our old friend, the ZOO file. To save the original ZOO file so we can use it later,

. use zoo

. copy to newzoo

00010 RECORDS COPIED

Enter the following commands as a command file as described at the beginning of this chapter. We'll call this new command file ZOOADD. It will append new records to the ZOO file.

```
use newzoo
set format to screen
set talk off
store 'C' to done
do while done = 'C' .or. done = 'c'
        erase
        append blank
        @ 5,5 say 'ANIMAL' get animal
        @ 7,5 say 'QUANTITY' get quantity
        @ 9,5 say 'DATE' get date
        @ 11,5 say 'CAGE NUMBER' get cage:no
        @ 13,5 say 'SEX' get sex
        @ 15,5 say 'VALUE' get value
        read
        @ 20,5 say 'USE "C" TO CONTINUE,'
        @ 21,5 say ' RETURN KEY ONLY TO QUIT'
        accept to done
enddo
set talk on
return
```

The SET TALK OFF command wasn't really required in this case, but it's good to develop the habit of using it. The RETURN at the end of the command file returns program operation to the process that called the file. In this case the file was called by a direct command, so we returned to the dBASE II prompt; but we could have been returned to another command file, as we'll see later on. The RETURN at the end of a file is not required, but putting it there is another good habit to get into.

To use the command file, type

. do zooadd

and then use

. list

to see the results.

You could also run the command file from the IBM PC operating system with

dbase zooadd

or from Apple CP/M with

dbase-ii zooadd

IF . . . ELSE

Sometimes it is useful to give your command file the capability of making another type of decision. It works like this:

IF

some condition is true

then

do something

ELSE

do something else

ENDIF

Here's an example of its use. This command file should be named ZOOEDIT. In the example, indentation is used to make the program logic easier to follow. This is not necessary though.

```
use newzoo
set format to screen
set talk off
store 'c' to done
do while done = 'c' .or. done = 'C'
        erase
        accept 'Animal to edit? ' to manimal
        go 1
        store n to found
        do while .not. eof
            if trim(animal) = manimal
                store y to found
                @ 4,5 say 'Animal?' get animal
                @ 6,5 say 'Quantity?' get quantity
                @ 8,5 say 'Date?' get date
                @ 10,5 say 'Cage number?' get cage:no
                @ 12,5 say 'Sex?' get sex
                @ 14,5 say 'Value?' get value
                read
                skip
            else
                skip
            endif
        enddo
        if .not. found
            @ 16,5 say manimal + ' not found'
        endif
        @ 18,5 say 'Use C to continue'
        @ 19,5 say 'or press RETURN to quit'
        accept to done
enddo
set talk on
return
```

The EOF in the DO WHILE statement means End Of File. The TRIM(ANIMAL) deletes any trailing spaces from the field variable ANIMAL so the MANIMAL value can match it. SKIP moves the record pointer through a data file in order. If the SKIP after the READ were left out of the command file, only the first match of ANIMAL and MANIMAL would be processed. The way it is written, both LIONs and TIGERs will be edited.

Now try it out and add some animals to the database. Then use LIST to verify that they're really there.

PROCEDURES (COMMAND FILES)

As mentioned earlier, it is possible to use a command file from another command file. The original calls the second file with the line

do <command file>

where <command file> is the command filename. This is the same method used to run a command file directly from dBASE II. When the called command file (sometimes called a PROCEDURE) reaches a RETURN statement, it goes back to the command file that called it and continues on the next line. You can nest several command files; that is, a file can call another file, which can call another file, and so on, as shown in Fig. 6-1.

LOOP

A LOOP command is available that causes the command file to return to the most recent DO WHILE. If there is no previous DO WHILE, you'll get a syntax

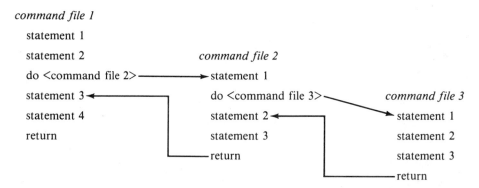

Fig. 6-1. Program flow through nested procedures (command files).

error. LOOP acts like the ENDDO statement but can be placed between the DO WHILE and the ENDDO. Using LOOP is quick and easy, but it can make a command file hard to understand. Usually there's a more graceful way to accomplish the same thing. Frequently you can use an IF . . . ELSE to avoid a LOOP. Here's an example using LOOP.

```
use newzoo
set talk off
set format to screen
accept 'Animal?' to manimal
do while .not. eof
        if trim(animal) <> manimal
            skip
            loop
        endif
        replace quantity with quantity + 1
        skip
enddo
set talk on
return
```

Instead, you can use

```
use newzoo
set talk off
set format to screen
accept 'Animal?' to manimal
do while .not. eof
        if trim(animal) = manimal
            replace quantity with quantity + 1
            skip
        else
            skip
        endif
```

enddo

set talk on

return

See how much easier it is to understand the second example, even though both examples do the same thing?

USING TWO DATABASES — PRIMARY AND SECONDARY

It's possible to have two databases open at the same time. Until now, we've opened each file in turn with the USE command. This closed any file that was USEd previously. The USE without a filename closed any file that was open.

Normally, any database file opened with USE is automatically set to PRIMARY. You don't have to do anything to make this happen. To open a SECONDARY (second) database file, use

select secondary

use <database file>

where <database file> is any database filename other than that used as the PRIMARY database. Use the SELECT SECONDARY statement *after* you open the PRIMARY database with USE. To return to the PRIMARY database file (the one opened before SELECT SECONDARY), use

select primary

To change the database file in either the PRIMARY or SECONDARY area, use the USE command after selecting that area. Furthermore, if you have just used SELECT SECONDARY and wish to refer to a field variable in the PRIMARY database, just prefix the PRIMARY field name with P., for example, P.QUANTITY. Likewise, if you have used SELECT PRIMARY, then use an S. prefix with the SECONDARY database's field name to refer to a field variable in the SECONDARY database.

The main advantage of using PRIMARY and SECONDARY databases is that you can keep your position in one database (usually the PRIMARY) while the other (SECONDARY) is in use. If you use USE instead of SELECT PRIMARY and SELECT SECONDARY to switch back and forth between two database files, the record pointer is set back to the first record every time you USE a database.

Chapter 7

Advanced Programming

FUNCTIONS

A *function* is an expression that returns a value. There are many useful functions available in dBASE II. So far you've seen a few of them; for example, STR and TRIM. Here is a complete list.

TYPE

If you wish to check the type of a variable, expression, or constant, you can use TYPE( ). It returns an N if the item is numeric, C if it's a character, and L if it's logical. If the variable doesn't exist, TYPE( ) returns a U for "undefined."

```
. store 'T' to letter
T
. ? type(letter)
C
. store T to letter
.T.
. ? type(letter)
L
. store 1234 to number
```

1234

. ? type(number)

N

The Integer Function — INT( )

The INT( ) function deletes any fractional value of any numeric expression within the parentheses. INT( ) truncates, or cuts off digits, it doesn't round.

. ? int(234.567)

234

. store 56.48 to num

56.48

. ? int(num)

56

. ? int(num + 1)

57

. ? int(-3.25)

-3

Did the last one surprise you? Remember, INT( ) always truncates. In Microsoft BASIC the INT function would return a -4 (it rounds down to the next lowest integer, whether it's positive or negative, instead of truncating).

The Record Number Function (#)

The character "#" stands for the present record number in the file in use or selected. Thus

. use zoo

. go 5

. ? #

5

. go top

. ? #

1

The String Function — STR( )

We've met the string function (STR) before. It converts a numeric variable to a character string, which can be stored in a character variable. The number of digits (including signs and decimal point) has to be included, together with the number of decimal places, just as it does when a database structure is set up. Thus

. store 123.456 to num

123.456

. ? str(num,7,3)

123.456

. ? str(num,5,1)

123.4

. store str(num,6,2) to string

123.45

. ? string

123.45

You've seen the STR( ) function used when index files were first discussed in Chapter 4, when we indexed using a numeric field. STR( ) is used like STR$( ) in BASIC.

The Substring Function — $( )

The substring function was treated in detail at the end of Chapter 3. Its use is summarized here.

The "$" character stands for the substring function.

. ? $('John Jones',2,3)

ohn

. store 1 to x

          1

. store 3 to y

          3

. store 'Bill Miller' to name

Bill Miller

. store $(name,x,y) to newname

Bil

. ? newname

Bil

As you can see, within the parentheses, the character expression comes first, then the numeric expression representing the start of the substring, and finally the numeric expression representing the length of the substring.

If the length expression exceeds the length of the string, only the characters available will be placed in the substring. Thus

. ? $('fortune',4,8)

tune

If this function is used to create a key for indexing, the start and length must be literals; that is, numeric constants — not expressions or variables. For instance, if you want to index a set of dates of the format MM/DD/YY by year, you can use

. index on $(date,7,2)

But you can't use the format

. index on $(date, x,y)

This is like MID$( ) in BASIC.

Converting a Numeric String to a Numeric Value — VAL( )

There are two ways to convert from a numeric string to a numeric value. One is to use the VAL( ) function. This converts from a numeric string to an integer value. Note that it only converts the integer portion of the number represented by the string. For example,

. ? val('123.456')

    123

. store val('123.456') to num

    123

. ? num

    123

. ? type(num)

N

. ? num + .5

    123.9

Note that the .456 was retained in num but not displayed. This can cause all sorts of grief. Remember it. VAL( ) converts only the leading numeric characters in the string, up to a nonnumeric character.

. ? val('321ABC5')

    321

This works the same way as the VAL( ) function does in BASIC, except that in BASIC, the decimal portion of the number is included and displayed; it is not converted to an integer display.

    If you wish to convert a string with a decimal point and also wish to retain the portion of the numeric value after the decimal point, use

. store '456.789' to num

456.789

. ? &num

456.789

. ? &num + .1

456.889

    The & is called the *macro symbol*. A macro of a variable treats the contents of the variable as though you had typed them directly in, rather than using the variable to represent them. Other ways to use macros include the following: First SET TALK OFF and SET TALK ON are stored as the macros TOFF and TON.

. store 'set talk off' to toff

set talk off

. store 'set talk on' to ton

set talk on

Then TOFF is called. The SET TALK OFF command stored in TOFF prevents the display of the action taken by the next store command.

. &toff

. store 123 to num

When TON is called, the SET TALK ON command causes action to be displayed again.

```
. &ton
. store 123 to num
123
```

RANK( )

The RANK function converts the first character of a string to its ASCII value. Here's an example.

```
. ? rank('ABC')
    65
```

Note that the ASCII value of only the first character in the string was printed, so the following code produces the same results:

```
. ? rank('A')
    65
```

This works the same way as the ASC( ) function in BASIC.

The Length Function (LEN)

To find the length of a string, use the LEN( ) function.

```
. ? len('abcde')
    5
. store 'fghijklmno' to string
fghijklmno
. ? len(string)
    10
```

This command does the same thing as LEN( ) in BASIC.

The Deleted Record Function — *

The deleted record function gives you a way to tell if a record has been deleted without LISTing or DISPLAYing it, thus:

. use zoo

. delete record 5

00001 DELETION(S)

. delete record 7

00001 DELETION(S)

. go 5

. ? *

.T.

. skip

RECORD: 00006

. ? *

.F.

. skip

RECORD: 00007

. ? *

.T.

The * is used to do the job. The

. ? *

statements in the listing above ask the question "Is this record deleted?" It will return .T. if the record is deleted; otherwise it will return .F. Here are some more examples.

. go 5

. store * to del

.T.

. ? del

.T.

. ? type(del)

L

. recall all

00002 RECALL(S)

In this last example, the statement

. store * to del

stores the "deleted" or "not deleted" status of a record in a variable called del.

The deleted record function is usually used in an IF or DO WHILE statement. For example,

. go 5

. if *

statement

statement

. endif

The End-of-File Function — EOF

We've been using EOF right along. EOF is a logical variable set by the system to return .T. when the end of a database file has been reached. You saw it in use in several command list examples in Chapter 6. It's usually used with an IF or DO WHILE statement. This same function is present in most versions of BASIC and other languages.

The Substring Search Function — @( )

Like the BASIC INSTR( ) function, the @ command is used to find the position of the first occurrence of a particular substring within a string. The result is numeric.

. ? @('b','abc')

    2

. store 'ASHTON-TATE' to db

ASHTON-TATE

. ? @('H',db)

    3

. ? @('TON',db)

    4

. ? @('Z',db)

    0

If the substring is found, the position of its first character within the string is returned; if it is not found, a 0 is returned.

The Uppercase Function — !( )

Sometimes you need to be sure that an operator's keyboard input is in the correct case, so matching can be accomplished. The easiest way is to force the input to uppercase, then match on an uppercase string. This example shows the lowercase to uppercase conversion process.

```
. store 'abcde' to lower
abcde
. store !(lower) to upper
ABCDE
. ? lower
abcde
. ? upper
ABCDE
```

The ! is the character chosen for the conversion function. In dBASE II, there is no command to go from uppercase to lowercase.

The Number-to-Character Function — CHR( )

The CHR command is the opposite of the RANK function. While RANK( ) returns the ASCII value of the first character in a string, CHR( ) returns the character when the ASCII value is given.

```
. ? chr(65)
A
. ? chr(97)
a
. ? chr(35)
#
```

This function can also be used to generate actions that are not represented by characters. Examples include 13, the carriage return; 10, the line feed; and 12, the form feed. The CHR$( ) function in BASIC is used the same way.

DATE( )

If you wish to display or print the system date, use DATE( ). The system date is that date given by the operator when the computer is started (PC-DOS or MS-DOS), or when dBASE II is started (CP/M). Assuming the date was entered as 5-23-84, then

. ? date( )

05/23/84

. store date( ) to day

05/23/84

. ? day

05/23/84

. set date to 12 25 83

. ? date( )

12/25/83

This example shows that DATE( ) can be used either to supply the date or to change the system date. Please note that there is never anything in the parentheses following DATE. They are only there so DATE( ) will not be confused with a variable you may call DATE.

FILE( )

Sometimes it is handy to be able to check for the existence of a file before you open it. If the file does not exist, perhaps the operator is using the wrong diskette, or maybe the command file program hasn't yet created that file; your command file can then take appropriate action instead of crashing (making an unscheduled termination). The FILE function is logical and returns .T. if the file exists, .F. if it does not.

. ? file('zoo')

.T.

TRIM( )

You've been using TRIM for some time. This function merely removes any trailing spaces from a string. It is usually used on a character field variable's value.

. use zoo

. 1

. ? animal

ant

. ? len(animal)

20

. ? len(trim(animal))

3

SET COMMANDS

Besides the few SET commands we've already discussed, there are many others. A complete list is covered here. As commands, all the words given are preceded by the word SET and followed by ON or OFF, as the programmer desires.

ECHO

SET ECHO is generally used for debugging a command file. It causes each command in the list to be displayed on the screen (or printed) as it is enacted. When ECHO is used together with the STEP command, it's easy to debug a command file. More information about debugging is given with the STEP command, treated next. To produce ECHO, use ON. The default is OFF.

STEP

SET STEP is generally used with ECHO. When the function is ON, the program stops after each statement in the command file. At that point you can issue a direct command (perhaps display the value in a variable at that point), leave the program (using the Escape key), or use the RETURN key to continue to the next step. To produce STEP, use ON. The default is OFF.

TALK

We encountered SET TALK in our discussion of macros (p. 99) before. It turns off the display of the results of commands such as STORE. To produce this effect, use OFF. The default is ON.

PRINT

When PRINT is set to ON, any output to the screen is also sent to the printer. The default is OFF. (See also "SET FORMAT TO PRINT" later in this chapter.)

CONSOLE

When CONSOLE is set to OFF, no output will be sent to the screen. The default is ON. The syntax is

. set console off

ALTERNATE

When set to ON, ALTERNATE is used to echo output to a disk file. See "SET ALTERNATE TO" on page 110 to find out how to designate the filename. The default is OFF.

You might want to use this feature to log the operation of your program if it does not seem to be running properly, or when you are testing the program. To use it use

. set alternate on

. set alternate to filename

where *filename* is the name of the file you wish to use.

SCREEN

Full-screen operations (using cursor control to move the cursor around the screen) for CREATE, EDIT, INSERT, and APPEND are turned on when SCREEN is set to ON, which is the default value. The command

. set screen off

would turn off the screen display. You might want to do this before printing, so that the print-out would be the only output.

LINKAGE

LINKAGE is an extremely useful command. When the command

. set linkage on

is used, moving the record pointer in either the PRIMARY or SECONDARY database file causes the record pointer in the other file to move also. It does not force the record pointers to point to identical record numbers, but moves both pointers the same number of records when either pointer is moved. This permits you to use 64 fields in a record, 32 in each database, which can be very useful if you need those extra fields. (There are ways to compress the data that would normally be stored in several fields so that it can be stored in a single field, but LINKAGE is simple to use.) With LINKAGE, you can also have two indexes in use at one time; very handy. Just be careful not to move one of the pointers with some other command without moving the other the same distance. The default is OFF.

COLON

When set to ON, COLON displays the colons indicating the field size after a GET command. ON is the default.

BELL

If that beep you hear every time you make a mistake annoys you, set BELL to OFF. The default is ON.

ESCAPE

To stop the Escape key (Esc) from functioning, use OFF. This will help you avoid program crashes that can happen when an inexperienced operator uses Esc either by design or by accident. The default is ON.

EXACT

When EXACT is turned ON, character strings must match exactly (except for trailing blanks) in the FIND command and the pattern string to be found. If EXACT is turned OFF, the characters to be matched must be the same and in the same position as in the pattern string, but the string being examined can have additional characters and still match. The default is OFF.

INTENSITY

Usually, full-screen operations will have dim and bright video, or standard and reverse video, depending on what you requested when you installed the system. To change this, set INTENSITY to OFF:

. set intensity off

You might wish to do this if you were annoyed by the bright characters, or found the characters to be too bright when the dim characters were set bright enough to be easily visible.

The default is ON.

DEBUG

If you turn DEBUG ON when using STEP and ECHO to debug a command file, the output from the STEP and ECHO commands will be sent to the printer instead of the screen. If the normal program output is set to go to the screen, it will go both to the screen and to the printer. This command gives you a hard copy of your debugging efforts and keeps the debugging output from messing up your nicely formatted display. The default is OFF.

CARRY

If you are appending new records and CARRY is turned ON, the data entered in all fields in the previous record will be passed along to the next. This is useful when some of the data remains the same from record to record. CARRY saves you the trouble of typing identical data in each time, for example, the city and state fields in a mailing list.

CONFIRM

You will remember that when you are entering data to EDIT or APPEND, for example, if a field is filled, dBASE II automatically jumps to the next field without a <RETURN>. If this is annoying and you find yourself using <RETURN> anyway, thus skipping a field, you may wish to disable this feature. To do so, set CONFIRM to ON. The default is OFF.

EJECT

Normally, REPORT will roll the paper to the beginning of a new page before it prints a report. This can waste a lot of paper. To avoid this automatic form feed, set EJECT to OFF. The default is ON.

RAW

When RAW is set to OFF, spaces are added between fields when the LIST and DISPLAY commands are used without including a list of fields in the command. When RAW is ON, the fields are placed as close to each other as the structure field size will allow on each line, with no added spaces between them for separation. The default is OFF.

DELETED

If you set DELETED to ON, deleted fields will be ignored by commands that can use the NEXT phrase — for example, FIND, LIST, LOCATE, and COUNT.

If DELETED is set to OFF, deleted records will be treated as undeleted by the FIND, LIST, LOCATE, and COUNT commands, but will be ignored (treated as deleted) by COPY and APPEND. The default is OFF.

SET TO COMMANDS

Each of these commands begins with SET and ends with TO and is followed by a setting.

SET HEADING TO

If you follow the SET HEADING TO with a string, for example

. set heading to 'WEEKLY REPORT'

that string will be printed on the REPORT header line.

SET FORMAT TO

SET FORMAT TO determines where the output of @ commands (SAY) will be sent. The options are SCREEN or PRINT. Thus, you can use

. set format to screen

This causes the line following SAY to be displayed on the screen.
Or use

. set format to print

to print the line following SAY.
One other option of this command lets you READ to the GET requests from a file. In this case, follow the word TO with the name of the file containing the responses:

. set format to b:answer

SET DEFAULT TO

If all your files are on a disk drive other than the one dBASE II is on, you have to remember to prefix all the filenames you use with that drive letter — A:, B:, C:, and so on. If you follow the SET DEFAULT TO command with a drive letter, with or without the colon, all filenames mentioned will then be automatically prefixed with that letter. Very handy.

Note: SET DEFAULT TO does not affect the CP/M or IBM DOS selected drive. This only affects drive names mentioned by the dBASE II user.

SET ALTERNATE TO

If you should wish to echo all interaction with dBASE II to a disk file (see "ALTERNATE" in the "SET Commands" section), you can select the name of the file to hold that data by entering it after the TO in SET ALTERNATE TO. Thus,

. set alternate to b:echofile

. set alternate on

will store data in a file called "echofile." The SET ALTERNATE ON command actually begins the echoing process.

SET DATE TO

To change the system date, follow SET DATE TO with the date (see Chapter 1). For example, use

. set date to 15/12/84

or

. set date to 15 12 84

or

. set date to 15,12,84

and so forth to set the date to December 15, 1985.

SET INDEX TO

You can set up to seven index files with this command, by following the TO with a list of index filenames. The first index filename mentioned is the master index file. This is the one used by such commands as FIND. Any index files that have been set before this command is used will be closed. If you use this command without any index filenames, all index files previously set will be closed. Thus

. set index to name, telnum, zip

sets three index files, with "name" being the master index file.

SET MARGIN TO

The SET MARGIN TO command sets the left margin for reports. Follow it with a numeric constant. All lines in the REPORT will be indented by that amount.

_____MERGING RECORDS WITH UPDATE_____

The following commands manipulate data in two files sometimes creating a third file.

UPDATE for Adding

First, UPDATE can be used for adding. It is assumed the fields to be added have the same name. Let's quickly CREATE a new database to illustrate this command. Use the following structure.

FILENAME: addzoo

001   cage:no,n,3

002   quantity,n,3

Now append these few records to the new database.

cage:no	quantity
5	1
4	2
3	3
2	4
1	5

Now copy the ZOO database to another file, so we don't foul up the original while doing this example. We want to keep the old ZOO database intact for future examples.

. use zoo

. copy to newzoo

00010 RECORDS COPIED

. use newzoo

. index on cage:no to cage

00010 RECORDS INDEXED

Now index the new ADDZOO database we just created.

. use addzoo

. index on cage:no to cageno

00005 RECORDS INDEXED

. use addzoo index cageno

. copy to temp

00005 RECORDS COPIED

. use temp

. copy to addzoo

00005 RECORDS COPIED

We could also have used SORT, but INDEX is quicker. Note that cage:no *must* be in ascending numerical order in the file.

Now we'll do the ADD.

. use newzoo index cage

. update from addzoo on cage:no add quantity

Notice that both databases were indexed on the same field, and that the index files were named differently. Also notice that both databases have a field QUANTITY structured the same way (numeric, three digits).

Now type LIST. You'll see that the USEd database, NEWZOO, had the QUANTITY from ADDZOO added to its QUANTITY. Cage numbers not mentioned in ADDZOO were not affected. You can list the original unchanged ZOO to see the difference between it and NEWZOO after NEWZOO was UPDATEd from ADDZOO.

Remember, both databases, NEWZOO and ADDZOO, have to be INDEXed on the same field (cage:no in this case), and both must have the designated numeric field (QUANTITY in this case) structured the same way.

You can have several numeric fields after ADD, separated by commas. All fields will be ADDed to the USEd database when the index keys (cage numbers, or cage:no, in this case) match.

Obviously, the indexed field must have unique (all different) entries, or the program won't be able to determine which records to add to. Our example wouldn't work if we indexed on the ANIMAL field (if it were in ADDZOO), because the names are not unique (we have two lions and two tigers in the NEWZOO database). The program would not be able to determine which of the two lion or tiger records to add to.

UPDATE for Replacing

We can use UPDATE to replace a field, too. Let's set up a new ADDZOO database. CREATE it with this structure.

FILENAME: addzoo

| 001 | cage:no,n,3 |
| 002 | value,n,7,2 |

Now APPEND the following data:

cage:no	value
10	.10
14	250.00
11	200.00

Now INDEX it.

. use addzoo

. index on cage:no to cageno

00003 RECORDS INDEXED

. use addzoo index cageno

. copy to temp

00003 RECORDS COPIED

. use temp

. copy to addzoo

00003 RECORDS COPIED

Now do the replacement.

. use zoo

. copy to newzoo

00010 RECORDS COPIED

. use newzoo

. index on cage:no to cage

00010 RECORDS INDEXED

. use newzoo index cage

. update from addzoo on cage:no replace value

This time when you LIST NEWZOO, you'll see that the old cage:no values have been replaced with those from the ADDZOO database.

As with ADD, you can have several fields following the REPLACE. With UPDATE the fields can be of any type: numeric, character, or logical. Of course, all the fields have to be in both databases.

Also, if you add RANDOM after the field name(s), the replacing database (ADDZOO in our examples) need not be indexed. However, with either ADD or UPDATE, the database receiving the replacements (NEWZOO in our examples) must be indexed.

One last version of UPDATE requires both databases to be indexed on the same field, but the field names being replaced in the two files can be different. *Don't* type this in.

update from addzoo on cage:no replace value with price

This command assumes that ADDZOO has a field called PRICE and that its structure is the same as the value field in NEWZOO (numeric, seven digits, two decimal places).

Application of UPDATE

All these UPDATE commands are useful to update a master file from other files. For example, an inventory file could be ADDed from a list of parts received, as long as both are indexed on the part number. Or a master inventory file could be REPLACEd from a file containing a list of price changes.

JOIN

The JOIN command combines data from two databases, PRIMARY and SECONDARY, and stores it in a third. For the example, first CREATE a new ADDZOO file with the following structure.

FILENAME: addzoo

001   animal,c,20

002   donated,c,25

Now APPEND the following to ADDZOO.

ANIMAL	DONATED
ant	John Jones
python	Mary Smith
tarantula	Frank Miller

Now use

. select secondary

. use addzoo

. select primary

. use zoo

. join to newzoo for s.animal = animal fields animal,

donated,cage:no

. use newzoo

. list

You'll see that the animals from ADDZOO whose animal field matched that in ZOO were added to NEWZOO. (The animal field was mentioned in the JOIN command as the selection criterion.) You also changed the SECONDARY database to NEWZOO when you entered USE NEWZOO and LIST.

JOIN works as follows. The first animal (mentioned in the JOIN command) in the PRIMARY database (ZOO) is searched for in the SECONDARY database (ADDZOO). If it's found, the fields animal, donated, and cage:no (mentioned in the JOIN command) are added to the new database (NEWZOO), also mentioned in the JOIN command. In this way, each animal in ZOO, in turn, is searched for in ADD-ZOO and all occurrences found are added to NEWZOO.

We have combined the fields mentioned in the JOIN command in the new database, if the matching criteria (ANIMAL fields in this case) match in the PRIMARY and SECONDARY databases. The zoo can now send letters containing the list in NEWZOO to the people who donated the new animals, so they can know which cage number to look for to see their donated animal.

To give one practical example, JOIN could also be used to combine a list of customer numbers and back-ordered items with a customer number, name, and address file, so that customers could be notified about back orders.

Note that if the matching criteria are too loose, you can generate a very, very large new database, perhaps much larger than you intended. Be sure you give some thought to your file structure and to the JOIN matching criteria before you use this command.

SAVE . . . RESTORE

As mentioned earlier, you can have only 64 memory variables in use at any one time. To SAVE memory variables to the file MEMSAVE so that their space can be used for other memory variables, use

. save to memsave

. release all

MEMSAVE is just an example of a filename. Any could be used. After the memory variables have been saved, the RELEASE ALL clears the memory space so that other memory variables can be used. You can recover the variables, but you must first clear any current memory variables.

. save to savemem

. release all

. restore from memsave

The SAVE command can be phrased to save only specific memory variables. For example,

. save to memsave all like m*

. release all like m*

would SAVE all the variables with "m" as the first letter. (See "Selective Listing" in Chapter 2 for more information about wildcards. See also "RELEASE" in Chapter 3.) Use

. display memory

to see the results of the previous commands, if you wish. You'll have to create some memory variables, and then experiment with SAVE and RELEASE.

FORMATTING

Formatted data can be used in several ways. The addition of PICTURE followed by the format pattern can be used to force specific types of data when you use GET.

The formatting symbols are as shown in Table 7-1.

For example,

. erase

. store '(000)000-0000' to telnum

(000)000-0000

. @ 5,1 say 'Input phone' get telnum picture '(999)999-9999'

. read

Table 7-1.   dBASE II formatting symbols

Symbol	Function
9	Accepts only digits
#	Accepts only digits and a period (.) to indicate decimal places
A	Accepts only alphabetic characters
!	Converts alphabetic characters to uppercase
X	Accepts any character
$	Shows dollar sign
*	Shows asterisk

The response is

Input phone :(000)000-0000:

Now only numerals (specified by the 9s) in the proper pattern will be accepted here. If (123)456-7890 was entered, then

. ? telnum

(123)456-7890

Note the extra (nonformatting) characters such as "-", "(", and ")" were also stored in the variable. Telnum is obviously now a character variable. To prove this,

. ? type(telnum)

C

Another example might be

. erase

. store '000 00 0000' to ssn

000 00 0000

. @ 5,1 say 'Social security number' get ssn picture '999 99 9999' or

    . erase

    . store '   ' to lname

    . @ 5,1 say 'Last name' get lname picture '!!!!!!!!!!'

    . read

which would limit the name to ten characters and automatically convert any lower-case letters entered to uppercase.

Or perhaps,

    . erase

    . store '   ' to partnum

    . @ 5,1 say 'Part number' get partnum picture 'A999A'

    . read

where the first and last characters of the part number must be alphabetic and the middle three must be digits, for a total of five characters.

And finally,

    . store ' / / ' to day

    / /

    . @ 5,1 say 'Date' get day picture '99/99/99'

    . read

which forces the proper date format. Of course, the operator can still put the year, day, and month digits in the wrong places!

Another use of these pictures is to print numbers in a column. For example,

    . set format to print

    . @ 1,20 say 1 using '9,999.00'

    . @ 2,20 say 5.2 using '9,999.99'

    . @ 3,20 say 1000 using '9,999.99'

    . @ 4,0

    . set format to screen

First of all, the SET FORMAT TO PRINT command sent any following output to the printer. You'll notice the numbers are printed in a nice even column:

    1.00

    5.20

1,000.00

Try it without the pictures to see the difference. Also try it without the @ 4,0. To print checks, you could use

. set format to print

. @ 1,10 say 1 using '$$,$$$.99'

. @ 2,10 say 5.2 using '$$,$$$.99'

. @ 3,10 say 1000 using '$$,$$$.99'

. @ 4,10

. set format to screen

$$$$1.00

$$$$5.20

$1,000.00

This makes the resulting checks harder to alter because there are no empty spaces between the dollar sign and the first digit of the amount.

It is important to note that when a PICTURE clause is used, the result is a string, even if it is a string of digits. That is, when PICTURE is used, the GET variable is of type STRING (or LOGICAL).

TEXT . . . ENDTEXT

Another interesting feature of dBASE II permits a quick way to produce form letters. Let's say you have a file called CUSTOMER with fields NAME, ADDRESS, and C:S:Z. You wish to tell these customers all about a gigantic sale you are having. The following command file would do it.

```
set format to print

use customer

do while .not. eof

        @ 1,30 say 'name'

        @ 2,30 say 'address'

        @ 3,30 say 'c:s:z'
```

```
        @ 5,5 say

        text

            Be sure to come in soon and take advantage of

        our gigantic diskette sale! As much as 3 percent

        off on some brands!

        endtext

        eject

        skip

    enddo

    set format to screen

    return
```

The EJECT command causes the printer to do a form feed (advance the paper to the top of the next page, if all goes as planned). The C:S:Z means city, state, and zip.

You can probably see many possibilities for using TEXT . . . ENDTEXT.

CASE

CASE is useful in many circumstances. For example, in a menu, CASE is easier to use than a long string of IF statements. Here's a sample menu operated by CASE statements. By the way, don't type this in; it won't run, because the called procedures do not exist.

```
    do while t

        ? '            MENU'

        ? '1: Add record'

        ? '2: Delete record'

        ? '3: Change record'

        ? '4: Search for record'

        ? '5: End program'

        ? 'YOUR CHOICE?'

        store '  ' to choice

        accept to choice
```

```
do case
    case choice  =  1
        do addrec
    case choice  =  2
        do delrec
    case choice  =  3
        do chgrec
    case choice  =  4
        do srchrec
    case choice  =  5
        erase
        return
    otherwise
            ? 'BAD CHOICE, TURKEY!'
            ? 'Press return key to continue'
        wait
    endcase
enddo
```

As you can see, the DOs send you to command files which, upon completion, return you to the menu. The RETURN takes you out of the DO WHILE T loop. The OTHERWISE clause (optional) gently tells the operator that an unwise choice was made. The DO WHILE T means continue to loop forever. However, before forever arrives, the operator can pick choice 5 to escape the loop.

Chapter 8

An Annotated Program

This chapter provides a sample program written as dBASE II command files. It is a working inventory program, complete with menus and most of the standard features. Annotation is provided for some of the lines that might be unclear. In some cases, the explanatory lines will be in the program, marked with a leading *; in other cases, the explanation is in the text following the program. All program entries are in uppercase, but you may use either uppercase or lowercase.

Remember, there are many ways you could put such a program together. The methods used here represent only one way to do it. The command files are written primarily to be easy to understand.

You'll find that it's really a simple project to put a program together. Soon you'll be writing your own applications.

CREATE A NEW DATABASE

For the purposes of illustration, we've just about run our ZOO database into the ground. It served its purpose as a simple database, but now we should have something a bit more complex to illustrate the use of a command file. For this, we'll set up an inventory database. It will have nine fields, and we'll call the database STOCK. Use the CREATE command to set up the following fields structure:

001   PART:NO,C,8

002   DESCRIPT,C,9

003   ON:HAND,N,4

004   REORDER,N,4

005   PRICE,N,7,2

006   COST,N,7,2

007   SUPPLIER,C,9

008   COMPUTER,C,9

009   ON:ORDER,N,4

Now let's assume we are selling computer programs. After you've written all the command files presented in this chapter, you'll enter the following 20 items into the STOCK file. Look at these items now to see the data the command files will be working on.

PART: NO	DESCRIPT	ON: HAND	RE- ORD	PRICE	COST	SUPPLIER	COM- PUTER	ON: ORDER
12.74	dBASE II	3	1	700.00	400.00	ASHTON	IBM	0
15.14	dBASE II	4	2	700.00	400.00	ASHTON	APPLE	0
15.23	QUICKCODE	3	1	295.00	200.00	FOX	APPLE	0
12.17	dGRAPH	2	1	295.00	200.00	FOX	IBM	0
15.29	VISICALC	4	2	400.00	295.00	VISICORP	APPLE	0
12.56	1-2-3	3	1	495.00	300.00	LOTUS	IBM	0
15.32	ZORK I	0	2	50.00	35.00	INFOCOM	APPLE	0
15.11	FROGGER	1	2	35.00	20.00	SIERRA	APPLE	0
12.07	FRIDAY	2	4	295.00	180.00	ASHTON	IBM	0
12.02	CBASIC	2	2	150.00	80.00	DIGITAL	IBM	0
12.15	CP/M 86	2	1	60.00	40.00	DIGITAL	IBM	0
12.31	WORD	1	2	375.00	200.00	MICROSOFT	IBM	0
12.14	FLIGHT	2	3	50.00	35.00	MICROSOFT	IBM	0
10.92	GEN LEG	1	1	495.00	300.00	BPI	LISA	0
15.87	DOS BOSS	2	3	25.00	15.00	BEAGLE	APPLE	0
15.85	DEADLINE	2	2	60.00	45.00	INFOCOM	APPLE	0
12.39	WORDSTAR	2	4	495.00	350.00	MICROPRO	IBM	0
20.14	SARGON II	2	1	50.00	35.00	HAYDEN	TRS-80	0
12.32	SYMPHONY	2	1	695.00	400.00	LOTUS	IBM	0
12.29	LATTICE C	1	1	500.00	300.00	LIFEBOAT	IBM	0

The PART:NO field would be the in-store reference number. The DESCRIPT field is the name of the program. The ON:HAND field is the number of programs in stock. The REORDER field is the level below which you wish to order replacement stock. The PRICE field is the retail price. The COST field is the wholesale price you pay for the program as a dealer. The SUPPLIER is the name (shortened) of the supplier of the program. (In reality, you'd probably order most programs from a single distributor.) The COMPUTER is the computer the program is formatted to run on. (In reality, most programs have versions for several computers.) The ON:ORDER tells you how many of the programs you've ordered but not yet received.

The next step is to CREATE another file containing the supplier's full name and address. We'll call this database SUPPLIER. It will have four fields.

001	SHORT,C,10
002	FULL,C,20
003	ADR,C,25
004	CITY,C,24

Once again, you'll enter the contents of the file using the command files you'll write. Glance at the following list now to see the types of data to be entered.

		ADR
SHORT	FULL	CITY
ASHTON	ASHTON-TATE	10150 W. JEFFERSON BLVD.
		CULVER CITY, CA 90230
FOX	FOX & GELLER	604 MARKET ST.
		ELMWOOD PARK, NJ 07407
VISICORP	VISICORP	2895 ZANKER RD.
		SAN JOSE, CA 95134
LOTUS	LOTUS DEVELOPMENT	161 FIRST ST.
		CAMBRIDGE, MA 02142
INFOCOM	INFOCOM INC.	55 WHEELER ST.
		CAMBRIDGE, MA 02138
SIERRA	SIERRA ON-LINE INC.	36575 MUDGE RANCH RD.
		COARSEGOLD, CA 93614
DIGITAL	DIGITAL RESEARCH	160 CENTRAL AVE.
		PACIFIC GROVE, CA 93950

MICROSOFT	MICROSOFT CORP.	10700 NORTHUP WAY
		BELLEVUE, WA 98004
BPI	BPI SYSTEMS	3423 GUADALUPE
		AUSTIN, TX 78705
BEAGLE	BEAGLE BROS.	4315 SIERRA VISTA
		SAN DIEGO, CA 92103
MICROPRO	MICROPRO INTER.	33 SAN PABLO AVE.
		SAN RAFAEL, CA 94903
HAYDEN	HAYDEN SOFTWARE CO.	600 SUFFOLK ST.
		LOWELL, MA 01853
LIFEBOAT	LIFEBOAT ASSOC.	1651 THIRD AVE.
		NEW YORK, NY 10028

The SHORT name is to match the SUPPLIER field in the STOCK database. The FULL, ADR, and CITY fields give the full name, address, city, state, and zip code of the supplier.

MENU

First we'll write the menu that calls all the command files. It too will be a command file. Its name will be MENU. Use

. MODIFY COMMAND MENU

to begin writing the MENU command file.

```
SET FORMAT TO SCREEN
SET TALK OFF
SET PRINT OFF
SET CONSOLE ON
DO WHILE T
STORE ' ' TO CHOICE
* 1 space
ERASE
```

```
@ 1,14 SAY 'MAIN MENU'
@ 3,5 SAY 'A: ADD NEW STOCK'
@ 4,5 SAY 'B: CHANGE RECORD'
@ 5,5 SAY 'C: DELETE PART NUMBER'
@ 6,5 SAY 'D: SEARCH INVENTORY'
@ 7,5 SAY 'E: PRINT INVENTORY'
@ 8,5 SAY 'F: ADD NEW SUPPLIER'
@ 9,5 SAY 'G: DELETE SUPPLIER'
@ 10,5 SAY 'H: CHANGE SUPPLIER'
@ 11,5 SAY 'I: PRINT SUPPLIER LIST'
@ 12,5 SAY 'J: REORDER REPORT'
@ 13,5 SAY 'K: END PROGRAM'
@ 15,5 SAY 'YOUR CHOICE BY LETTER? ' GET CHOICE PICTURE 'A'
READ
STORE !(CHOICE) TO CHOICE
DO CASE
CASE CHOICE = 'A'
  DO ADDSTOCK
CASE CHOICE = 'B'
  DO CNGSTOCK
CASE CHOICE = 'C'
  DO DELSTOCK
CASE CHOICE = 'D'
  DO SEARCH
CASE CHOICE = 'E'
  DO PRINTINV
CASE CHOICE = 'F'
  DO ADDSUP
CASE CHOICE = 'G'
  DO DELSUP
CASE CHOICE = 'H'
```

```
        DO CNGSUP
      CASE CHOICE = 'I'
        DO PRINTSUP
    CASE CHOICE = 'J'
        DO REORDER
    CASE CHOICE = 'K'
        ERASE
        SET TALK ON
        RELEASE ALL
        QUIT
      OTHERWISE
        @ 17,5 SAY 'TRY AGAIN WITH A LETTER FROM A TO K'
        @ 18,5 SAY 'PRESS RETURN TO CONTINUE'
        WAIT
      ENDCASE
    ENDDO WHILE T
```

The first four SET statements make sure that everything is set up properly to run the program. You may wish to add others from the SET list in Chapter 7, perhaps SET CONFIRM ON, for example.

The DO WHILE T creates an infinite loop. It will continue to run until menu choice K:END PROGRAM is selected. This is the only way out of the loop.

The first 12 SAY statements put the menu on the screen. The one at 15,5 gets the user's choice. Note the PICTURE; it ensures that only a single letter will be accepted.

The READ command accepts the user's input.

We then use the !( ) function to convert the operator's response to uppercase, if it isn't already.

The CASE block tells dBASE II what to do if a valid choice has been made. The DOs call the appropriate command files to accomplish the menu choices.

The statements after OTHERWISE take care of an invalid choice. These lines will never be reached if a valid choice is made.

The WHILE T after ENDDO is for the programmer's benefit. The program doesn't try to act on it; it serves only to remind the programmer which WHILE or IF loop it refers to.

ADDING STOCK RECORDS

The next command file will permit adding new records to the STOCK database. Start with MODIFY COMMAND ADDSTOCK and write this file:

```
USE STOCK
IF .NOT. FILE('PARTNUM.NDX')
   INDEX ON PART:NO TO PARTNUM
ENDIF
USE STOCK INDEX PARTNUM
DO WHILE T
   ERASE
   STORE '        ' TO MNUM
   * 8 spaces
   @ 1,5 SAY 'ADD A PART NUMBER'
   @ 3,5 SAY 'PART NUMBER? ' GET MNUM PICTURE   '99.99999'
   @ 4,5 SAY 'USE RETURN TO QUIT'
   READ
   IF MNUM = '  .     '
      * 2 spaces, period, 5 spaces
      ERASE
      RELEASE ALL EXCEPT CHOICE
      RETURN
   ENDIF
   FIND &MNUM
   IF # = 0
      STORE '         ' TO MDESC
      * 9 spaces
      STORE 0 TO MONHAND
      STORE 0 TO MREORDER
      STORE 0.00 TO MPRICE
      STORE 0.00 TO MCOST
```

```
STORE '         ' TO MSUPP
* 9 spaces
STORE '         ' TO MCOMP
* 9 spaces
STORE 0 TO MONORD
@ 6,5 SAY 'DESCRIPTION' GET MDESC PICTURE 'XXXXXXXX'
@ 7,5 SAY 'ON HAND' GET MONHAND
@ 8,5 SAY 'REORDER LEVEL' GET MREORDER
@ 9,5 SAY 'PRICE' GET MPRICE
@ 10,5 SAY 'COST' GET MCOST
@ 11,5 SAY 'SUPPLIER' GET MSUPP PICTURE 'XXXXXXXX'
@ 12,5 SAY 'COMPUTER' GET MCOMP PICTURE 'XXXXXXXX'
@ 13,5 SAY 'ON ORDER' GET MONORD
STORE 'N' TO OK
@ 14,5 SAY 'ALL OK? (Y/N) ' GET OK PICTURE 'A'
READ
STORE !(OK) TO OK
IF OK <> 'Y'
   LOOP
ENDIF
APPEND BLANK
REPLACE PART:NO WITH MNUM
REPLACE DESCRIPT WITH MDESC
REPLACE ON:HAND WITH MONHAND
REPLACE REORDER WITH MREORDER
REPLACE PRICE WITH MPRICE
REPLACE COST WITH MCOST
REPLACE SUPPLIER WITH MSUPP
REPLACE COMPUTER WITH MCOMP
REPLACE ON:ORDER WITH MONORD
ELSE
```

```
@ 6,5 SAY 'PART NUMBER ALREADY IN FILE'
@ 8,5 SAY 'PRESS RETURN TO CONTINUE'
WAIT
ENDIF # = 0
ENDDO WHILE T
```

It takes a lot of typing but the program logic is clear. Enter each line in the program as a separate line when entering the command file. You can ignore the indentations. Remember, any line beginning with an asterisk (*) is a remark, so dBASE II ignores that line.

Here's how the program functions. First we USE the STOCK database. Next we check to see if the part number index file (PARTNUM) already exists. It may not if we're running the program for the first time. If it doesn't exist, we create it.

Next we USE the database with the PARTNUM index file.

The ERASE after DO WHILE T clears the screen.

We get a part number. We had preset the part number to seven blanks and the decimal point; we now check to see if it still contains the preset value after the operator has had the opportunity to enter the part number. If so, no part number was entered, and we return to the menu via the return statement. This is the only way out of this file. We retain the CHOICE variable for the menu CASE statement, which is still to be executed.

If we are still plodding along, we try to FIND the part number in the STOCK file. Notice that we use the ampersand (&) to pull out the contents of the memory variable MNUM. If the part number is there, the record number (# function) will not be 0.

If the part number was NOT found (# = 0), we enter a new record for that part number. To do this we preset all the GET variables O's and blank spaces with STORE commands. We use SAY . . . GETs to get the data from the operator. Then we ask if everything is OK. This is the operator's opportunity to change his or her mind. If the response is not Y, we LOOP back to the DO WHILE T and try again.

We use all the M variables to store the data in case the operator decides to back out after the data is entered. That way nothing is stored in the field variables. It's not a good idea to store entries in field variables unless we definitely intend to put them in the record.

The READ statement accepts "Y" or "N" in response to the "ALL OK?" prompt. If the operator has answered with "Y," we APPEND a blank record to receive the new data, and then use a series of REPLACEs to actually put the data into the new record. The ELSE part of the IF # = 0 statement tells the operator that the part number already exists. No data is solicited. We revert back to the DO WHILE T and try again, hoping for a valid part number from the operator this time around.

The ERASE after the DO WHILE T clears the screen and erases the GET variables for a new record.

Again, the information after ENDIF and ENDDO is for the programmer only; dBASE II ignores it.

CHANGING STOCK RECORDS

Use .MODIFY COMMAND CNGSTOCK to write the next command file. This file is used to change the data in a part number record.

```
USE STOCK
IF .NOT. FILE('PARTNUM.NDX')
   INDEX ON PART:NO TO PARTNUM
ENDIF
USE STOCK INDEX PARTNUM
DO WHILE T
   ERASE
   STORE '  .     ' TO MNUM
   * 2 spaces, decimal point, 5 spaces
   @ 1,5 SAY 'CHANGE A PART NUMBER RECORD'
   @ 3,5 SAY 'PART NUMBER? 'GET MNUM PICTURE '99.99999'
   @ 4,5 SAY 'PRESS RETURN TO QUIT'
   READ
   IF MNUM = '  .     '
      * 2 spaces, decimal point, 5 spaces
      ERASE
      RELEASE ALL EXCEPT CHOICE
      RETURN
   ENDIF
   FIND &MNUM
   IF # <> 0
      STORE DESCRIPT TO MDESC
      STORE ON:HAND TO MONHAND
```

```
STORE REORDER TO MREORDER
STORE PRICE TO MPRICE
STORE COST TO MCOST
STORE SUPPLIER TO MSUPP
STORE COMPUTER TO MCOMP
STORE ON:ORDER TO MONORD
@ 6,5 SAY 'DESCRIPTION ' GET MDESC PICTURE 'XXXXXXXX'
@ 7,5 SAY 'ON HAND ' GET MONHAND
@ 8,5 SAY 'REORDER LEVEL' GET MREORDER
@ 9,5 SAY 'PRICE' GET MPRICE
@ 10,5 SAY 'COST' GET MCOST
@ 11,5 SAY 'SUPPLIER' GET MSUPP PICTURE 'XXXXXXXX'
@ 12,5 SAY 'COMPUTER' GET MCOMP PICTURE 'XXXXXXXX'
@ 13,5 SAY 'ON ORDER' GET MONORD
@ 15,5 SAY 'ENTER CHANGES'
STORE 'N' TO OK
@ 17,5 SAY 'ALL OK? (Y/N) ' GET OK PICTURE 'A'
READ
STORE !(OK) TO OK
IF OK <> 'Y'
   LOOP
ENDIF
REPLACE PART:NO WITH MNUM
REPLACE DESCRIPT WITH MDESC
REPLACE ON:HAND WITH MONHAND
REPLACE REORDER WITH MREORDER
REPLACE PRICE WITH MPRICE
REPLACE COST WITH MCOST
REPLACE SUPPLIER WITH MSUPP
REPLACE COMPUTER WITH MCOMP
REPLACE ON:ORDER WITH MONORD
```

```
    ELSE
       @ 6,5 SAY 'PART NUMBER NOT IN FILE'
       @ 8,5 SAY 'PRESS RETURN TO CONTINUE'
       WAIT
    ENDIF # <> 0
 ENDDO WHILE T
```

This works a lot like the previous module, as you can see. But IF works just the opposite of the way it did before; this time we are looking for the presence, not the absence, of the part number in the file. Also, we store the field variables in the GET variables before we let the operator do the editing. Again, this is to avoid putting any data into the field variables before we are ready to STORE them in the record.

DELETING STOCK RECORDS

Use

. MODIFY COMMAND DELSTOCK

to name this file DELSTOCK.

```
USE STOCK
IF .NOT. FILE('PARTNUM.NDX')
   INDEX ON PART:NO TO PARTNUM
ENDIF
USE STOCK INDEX PARTNUM
DO WHILE T
   ERASE
   STORE '  .     ' TO MNUM
   * 2 spaces, decimal point, 5 spaces
   @ 1,5 SAY 'DELETE A PART NUMBER RECORD'
   @ 3,5 SAY 'PART NUMBER? ' GET MNUM PICTURE '99.99999'
   @ 4,5 SAY 'USE RETURN TO QUIT'
   READ
   IF MNUM = '  .     '
```

```
* 2 spaces, decimal point, 5 spaces
ERASE
RELEASE ALL EXCEPT CHOICE
RETURN
ENDIF
FIND &MNUM
IF # <> 0
   @ 6,5 SAY 'PART NUMBER ' + PART:NO
   @ 7,5 SAY 'DESCRIPTION ' + DESCRIPT
   @ 8,5 SAY 'ON HAND ' + STR(ON:HAND,4)
   @ 9,5 SAY 'REORDER LEVEL ' + STR(REORDER,4)
   @ 10,5 SAY 'PRICE ' + STR( PRICE,7,2)
   @ 11,5 SAY 'COST ' + STR(COST,7,2)
   @ 12,5 SAY 'SUPPLIER ' + SUPPLIER
   @ 13,5 SAY 'COMPUTER ' + COMPUTER
   @ 14,5 SAY 'ON ORDER ' + STR(ON:ORDER,4)
   STORE 'N' TO OK
   @ 17,5 SAY 'DELETE THIS RECORD? (Y/N) ' GET OK PICTURE 'A'
   READ
   STORE !(OK) TO OK
   IF OK <> 'Y'
      LOOP
   ENDIF
   DELETE
   PACK
   @ 18,5 SAY 'RECORD DELETED'
   STORE 1 TO PAUSE
   DO WHILE PAUSE < 50
      STORE PAUSE + 1 TO PAUSE
   ENDDO
```

```
  ELSE
    @ 6,5 SAY 'PART NUMBER NOT IN FILE'
    @ 8,5 SAY 'PRESS RETURN TO CONTINUE'
  WAIT
ENDIF # <> 0
ENDDO WHILE T
```

In this file we follow past procedure to check for the index file and GET the part number, RETURNing if no part number is entered. Then, as usual, we use FIND to locate the record. If the record is found, we display it on the screen and ask the operator if that is the proper record to delete. If so, we DELETE it and PACK the STOCK database. Then we go back for another record number. The DO WHILE loop after PACK is used as a delay, to give the operator time to read the RECORD DELETED message. You could change the program to let the operator decide whether to PACK the file.

This time we use the field variables to display the data rather than using memory variables, as there's no way for the operator to change the values in these variables.

If the part number is not found, we notify the operator as we have done in the other command files, and go back to get another part number.

_____SEARCHING STOCK RECORDS_____

We will use two command files to search the STOCK records. The first will set up the search criteria. We'll call it SRCHDATA. The second file will do the actual searching. We'll call it SEARCH.

First, use

```
. MODIFY COMMAND SRCHDATA
```

to set up the SRCHDATA command file.

```
ERASE
STORE F TO FOUND
STORE '  ' TO STRING
DO WHILE .NOT. FOUND
  ? 'SEARCH FOR WHAT DATA?'
  ?
```

```
? 'A: PART NUMBER'
? 'B: DESCRIPTION'
? 'C: ON HAND'
? 'D: REORDER'
? 'E: PRICE'
? 'F: COST'
? 'G: SUPPLIER'
? 'H: COMPUTER'
? 'I: ON ORDER'
? 'J: DONE'
?
? 'YOUR CHOICE BY LETTER?'
ACCEPT TO CHOOSE
STORE !(CHOOSE) TO CHOOSE
DO CASE
   CASE CHOOSE = 'A'
      STORE T TO FOUND
      STORE 'PART:NO' TO STRING
   CASE CHOOSE = 'B'
      STORE T TO FOUND
      STORE 'DESCRIPT' TO STRING
   CASE CHOOSE = 'C'
      STORE T TO FOUND
      STORE 'ON:HAND' TO STRING
   CASE CHOOSE = 'D'
      STORE T TO FOUND
      STORE 'REORDER' TO STRING
   CASE CHOOSE = 'E'
      STORE T TO FOUND
      STORE 'PRICE' TO STRING
```

```
   CASE CHOOSE = 'F'
     STORE T TO FOUND
     STORE 'COST' TO STRING
   CASE CHOOSE = 'G'
     STORE T TO FOUND
     STORE 'SUPPLIER' TO STRING
   CASE CHOOSE = 'H'
     STORE T TO FOUND
     STORE 'COMPUTER' TO STRING
   CASE CHOOSE = 'I'
     STORE T TO FOUND
     STORE 'ON:ORDER' TO STRING
   CASE CHOOSE = 'J'
     STORE T TO FOUND
   OTHERWISE
     ?
     ? 'NOT A VALID CHOICE, USE A LETTER FROM A THROUGH J'
     ? 'PRESS RETURN TO CONTINUE'
     WAIT
   ENDCASE
ENDDO WHILE .NOT. FOUND
IF CHOOSE = 'J'
   RETURN
ENDIF
   STORE F TO FOUND
   DO WHILE .NOT. FOUND
     ? 'MAKE A SELECTION OF TYPE OF COMPARISON'
     ?
     ? 'A: EQUAL'
     ? 'B: NOT EQUAL'
```

```
? 'C: GREATER THAN'
? 'D: LESS THAN'
? 'E: GREATER THAN OR EQUAL'
? 'F: LESS THAN OR EQUAL'
?
? 'CHOOSE BY LETTER'
ACCEPT TO COMP
STORE !(COMP) TO COMP
DO CASE
  CASE COMP = 'A'
    STORE T TO FOUND
    STORE STRING + ' = ' TO STRING
  CASE COMP = 'B'
    STORE T TO FOUND
    STORE STRING + ' <> ' TO STRING
  CASE COMP = 'C'
    STORE T TO FOUND
    STORE STRING + ' > ' TO STRING
  CASE COMP = 'D'
    STORE T TO FOUND
    STORE STRING + ' < ' TO STRING
  CASE COMP = 'E'
    STORE T TO FOUND
    STORE STRING + ' >= ' TO STRING
  CASE COMP = 'F'
    STORE T TO FOUND
    STORE STRING + ' <= ' TO STRING
  OTHERWISE
    ? 'NOT A VALID CHOICE, USE A LETTER FROM A THROUGH F'
    ? 'PRESS RETURN TO CONTINUE'
    WAIT
```

```
    ENDCASE
ENDDO WHILE .NOT. FOUND
ERASE
@ 1,1 SAY 'CHOOSE DATA TO SEARCH FOR'
IF CHOOSE = 'A' .OR. CHOOSE ='B' .OR. CHOOSE = 'G' .OR.
CHOOSE = 'H'
    STORE '           ' TO DATA
    * 9 spaces
    @ 3,1 SAY 'ENTER DATA' GET DATA
    READ
    STORE " ' " + TRIM(DATA) + " ' " TO DATA
ELSE
    STORE '           ' TO DATA
    * 7 spaces
    @ 2,1 SAY 'BE SURE IT IS A NUMBER' GET NUM
    READ
    STORE TRIM(NUM) TO DATA
ENDIF
STORE STRING + DATA TO STRING
RETURN
```

What we are doing is setting up a string in the memory variable STRING, which sets up the search criteria. The first WHILE loop is used to GET the user's choice of criteria. The field variable name that corresponds to the user's choice is put in STRING by the CASE statement, and FOUND is set to T. This will end the WHILE loop.

The second WHILE loop is used to GET the type of comparison. It works the same way as the first WHILE loop.

Finally, we get the type of data to compare to. Note that we make sure we GET the right kind of data with the statement that begins IF CHOOSE = 'A' . . . . It would not do to compare characters with a numeric field.

Finally, we end up with the comparison in the STRING variable.

Now use

. MODIFY COMMAND SEARCH

to start the command file SEARCH, which will use the SRCHDATA file.

```
USE STOCK
ERASE
STORE 0 TO COUNTER
STORE F TO DONE
IF .NOT. FILE('PARTNUM.NDX')
  INDEX ON PART:NO TO PARTNUM
ENDIF
USE STOCK INDEX PARTNUM
STORE 'N' TO PRINTCH
@ 1,5 SAY 'PRINT RESULTS? (Y/N)' GET PRINTCH PICTURE 'A'
READ
STORE !(PRINTCH) TO PRINTCH
DO WHILE (.NOT. DONE) .AND. COUNTER < 3
  DO SRCHDATA
  IF CHOOSE = 'J'
    STORE T TO DONE
  ELSE
    IF COUNTER = 0
      STORE STRING TO COMPARE
    ELSE
      STORE COMPARE + ' .AND. ' + STRING TO COMPARE
    ENDIF COUNTER = 0
    STORE COUNTER + 1 TO COUNTER
  ENDIF
ENDDO
IF COUNTER = 0
  ? 'NO COMPARISON DATA ENTERED'
  ? 'PRESS RETURN TO CONTINUE'
  WAIT
  ERASE
  RELEASE ALL EXCEPT CHOICE
```

```
    RETURN
ENDIF
ERASE
IF PRINTCH = 'Y'
   SET PRINT ON
ENDIF
DISPLAY ALL FOR &COMPARE
SET PRINT OFF
?
? 'PRESS RETURN TO CONTINUE'
WAIT
RELEASE ALL EXCEPT CHOICE
RETURN
```

Unless CHOOSE is DONE sooner, the SRCHDATA file will be called three times, so the user can search with up to three data relationships — for example,

PART:NO < 'A000Z' .AND. ON:HAND >50

   .AND. COMPUTER = 'ASTRAL'

Once we get the comparison criteria with the SRCHDATA command file, the rest is "duck soup."

First we see if the operator wants the results sent to the printer. Then a macro calls the concatenated condition out of memory to use with the DISPLAY ALL command. If the printer is set on, the output will be printed, too.

Using .OR. for the comparisons would be more difficult, but you might wish to explore the possibility of adding this feature. Don't forget, you will probably need to include grouping parentheses to clarify the conditional statement if you try to do this.

INVENTORY PRINTOUT

First you'll have to fill in dBASE II's REPORT form. If you need any help, refer to Chapter 5. The report should be named STOCKRPT. Here's one way to do it.

ENTER OPTIONS, M = LEFT MARGIN, L = LINES/PAGE,

   W = PAGE WIDTH: M = 0, L = 55, W = 80

PAGE HEADING? (Y/N) y

ENTER PAGE HEADING: INVENTORY REPORT

DOUBLE SPACE REPORT? (Y/N) n

ARE TOTALS REQUIRED? (Y/N) n

COL   WIDTH,CONTENTS

001   9,PART:NO

ENTER HEADING: PART NUMBER

002   10,DESCRIPT

ENTER HEADING: DESC.

003   5,ON:HAND

ENTER HEADING: ON HAND

004   6,REORDER

ENTER HEADING: RE ORDER

005   8,PRICE

ENTER HEADING: PRICE

006   8,COST

ENTER HEADING: COST

007   10,SUPPLIER

ENTER HEADING: SUPPLIER

008   10,COMPUTER

ENTER HEADING: COMPUTER

009   5,ON:ORDER

ENTER HEADING: ON ORDER

010   <RETURN>

The command file should be named PRINTINV. Here it is.

```
USE STOCK
IF .NOT. FILE('PARTNUM.NDX')
  INDEX ON PART:NO TO PARTNUM
ENDIF
USE STOCK INDEX PARTNUM
```

```
ERASE

@ 10,5 SAY 'SET PRINTER TO TOP OF PAGE'

@ 12,5 SAY 'PRESS RETURN TO CONTINUE'

WAIT

REPORT FORM STOCKRPT TO PRINT

RETURN
```

That's it! If you ever want to redo the report, use your DOS to delete the file STOCKRPT.FRM. Then run PRINTINV again from the menu.

ADDING A NEW SUPPLIER

Now we'll write some files to permit us to work with the SUPPLIER database. The first file lets us add new records. Name it ADDSUP.

```
USE SUPPLIER

IF .NOT. FILE('SHORTNME.NDX')

   INDEX ON SHORT TO SHORTNME

ENDIF

USE SUPPLIER INDEX SHORTNME

DO WHILE T

   ERASE

   STORE '          ' TO MSHORT

   * 10 spaces

   @ 1,5 SAY 'ADD A SUPPLIER'

   @ 3,5 SAY 'SHORT NAME? ' GET MSHORT PICTURE 'XXXXXXXXXX'

   @ 4,5 SAY 'USE RETURN TO QUIT'

   READ

   IF MSHORT = '          '

      * 10 spaces

      ERASE

      RELEASE ALL EXCEPT CHOICE

      RETURN
```

```
ENDIF
FIND &MSHORT
IF # = 0
   STORE '                ' TO MFULL
   * 20 spaces
   STORE '                 ' TO MADR
   * 25 spaces
   STORE '                ' TO MCITY
   * 24 spaces
   @ 6,5 SAY 'FULL NAME' GET MFULL PICTURE
'XXXXXXXXXXXXXXXXXXXX'
   @ 7,5 SAY 'ADDRESS' GET MADR PICTURE
'XXXXXXXXXXXXXXXXXXXXXXXXX'
   @ 8,5 SAY 'CITY, STATE, ZIP' GET MCITY PICTURE
'XXXXXXXXXXXXXXXXXXXXXXXX'
   STORE 'N' TO OK
   @ 17,5 SAY 'ALL OK? (Y/N) ' GET OK PICTURE 'A'
   READ
   STORE !(OK) TO OK
   IF OK <> 'Y'
      LOOP
   ENDIF
   APPEND BLANK
   REPLACE SHORT WITH MSHORT
   REPLACE FULL WITH MFULL
   REPLACE ADR WITH MADR
   REPLACE CITY WITH MCITY
ELSE
   @ 6,5 SAY 'SHORT NAME ALREADY IN FILE'
   @ 8,5 SAY 'PRESS RETURN TO CONTINUE'
   WAIT
ENDIF # = 0
ENDDO WHILE T
```

This is just the same as adding a record to the STOCK file. Only the GET and field variable names have been changed.

DELETING A SUPPLIER

This command file should be called DELSUP.

```
USE SUPPLIER
IF .NOT. FILE('SHORTNME.NDX')
   INDEX ON SHORT TO SHORTNME
ENDIF
USE SUPPLIER INDEX SHORTNME
DO WHILE T
   ERASE
   STORE '          ' TO MSHORT
   * 10 spaces
   @ 1,5 SAY 'DELETE A SUPPLIER'
   @ 3,5 SAY 'SHORT NAME? 'GET MSHORT PICTURE 'XXXXXXXXXX'
   @ 4,5 SAY 'USE RETURN TO QUIT'
   READ
   IF MSHORT = '          '
      * 10 spaces
      ERASE
      RELEASE ALL EXCEPT CHOICE
      RETURN
   ENDIF
   FIND &MSHORT
   IF # <> 0
      @ 6,5 SAY 'FULL NAME ' + FULL
      @ 7,5 SAY 'ADDRESS ' + ADR
      @ 8,5 SAY 'CITY, STATE, ZIP ' + CITY
      STORE 'N' TO OK
```

```
@ 17,5 SAY 'DELETE THIS RECORD ' GET OK PICTURE 'A'
READ
STORE !(OK) TO OK
IF OK <> 'Y'
   LOOP
ENDIF
DELETE
PACK
@ 14,5 SAY 'RECORD DELETED'
STORE 1 TO PAUSE
DO WHILE PAUSE < 50
   STORE PAUSE + 1 TO PAUSE
ENDDO
ELSE
   @ 6,5 SAY 'SHORT NAME NOT IN FILE'
   @ 8,5 SAY 'PRESS RETURN TO CONTINUE'
   WAIT
ENDIF # <> 0
ENDDO WHILE T
```

This works the same way as deleting a STOCK record, described earlier in the chapter.

CHANGING SUPPLIERS

Name this command file CNGSUP.

```
USE SUPPLIER
IF .NOT. FILE('SHORTNME.NDX')
   INDEX ON SHORT TO SHORTNME
ENDIF
USE SUPPLIER INDEX SHORTNME
DO WHILE T
```

```
ERASE
STORE '          ' TO MSHORT
* 10 spaces
@ 1,5 SAY 'CHANGE A SUPPLIER'
@ 3,5 SAY 'SHORT NAME? ' GET MSHORT PICTURE 'XXXXXXXXX'
@ 4,5 SAY 'USE RETURN TO QUIT'
READ
IF MSHORT = '          '
   * 10 spaces
   ERASE
   RELEASE ALL EXCEPT CHOICE
   RETURN
ENDIF
FIND &MSHORT
IF # <> 0
   STORE FULL TO MFULL
   STORE ADR TO MADR
   STORE CITY TO MCITY
   @ 6,5 SAY 'FULL NAME' GET MFULL PICTURE
'XXXXXXXXXXXXXXXXXXX'
   @ 7,5 SAY 'ADDRESS' GET MADR PICTURE
'XXXXXXXXXXXXXXXXXXXXXXXXX'
   @ 8,5 SAY 'CITY, STATE, ZIP' GET MCITY PICTURE
'XXXXXXXXXXXXXXXXXXXXXXXX'
   STORE 'N' TO OK
   @ 17,5 SAY 'ALL OK? (Y/N) ' GET OK PICTURE 'A'
   READ
   STORE !(OK) TO OK
   IF OK <> 'Y'
      LOOP
   ENDIF
```

```
        REPLACE SHORT WITH MSHORT

        REPLACE FULL WITH MFULL

        REPLACE ADR WITH MADR

        REPLACE CITY WITH MCITY

    ELSE

        @ 6,5 SAY 'SHORT NAME NOT IN FILE'

        @ 8,5 SAY 'PRESS RETURN TO CONTINUE'

        WAIT

    ENDIF # <> 0

ENDDO WHILE T
```

This works the same as changing a STOCK record, described earlier.

PRINTING THE SUPPLIER LIST

As with the INVENTORY PRINTOUT file, you'll first have to use the dBASE II REPORT feature to fill out the report form. Now generate the REPORT form. Call it SUPPRPT. Refer to Chapter 5 if necessary. Here's one way to do it.

ENTER OPTIONS, M = LEFT MARGIN, L = LINES/PAGE,

    W = PAGE WIDTH: M = 0,L = 55,W = 80

PAGE HEADING? (Y/N) y

ENTER PAGE HEADING: SUPPLIER LIST

DOUBLE SPACE REPORT? (Y/N) n

ARE TOTALS REQUIRED? (Y/N) n

COL   WIDTH,CONTENTS

001   11,SHORT

ENTER HEADING: SHORT NAME

002   15,FULL

ENTER HEADING: FULL NAME

003   26,ADR

ENTER HEADING: ADDRESS

004   25,CITY

ENTER HEADING: CITY STATE ZIP

005   <RETURN>

The following command file should be named PRINTSUP.

```
USE SUPPLIER
IF .NOT. FILE('SHORTNME.NDX')
   INDEX ON SHORT TO SHORTNME
ENDIF
USE SUPPLIER INDEX SHORTNME
SET EJECT OFF
ERASE
@ 10,5 SAY 'SET PRINTER TO TOP OF PAGE'
@ 12,5 SAY 'PRESS RETURN TO CONTINUE'
WAIT
REPORT FORM SUPPRPT TO PRINT
SET EJECT ON
RETURN
```

This works the same as the INVENTORY PRINTOUT file described earlier.

THE REORDERING REPORT

This is one of the trickier command files. In it we'll access both the STOCK and SUPPLIER databases. Name this command file REORDER.

```
USE STOCK
IF .NOT. FILE('PARTNUM.NDX')
   INDEX ON PART:NO TO PARTNUM
ENDIF
USE STOCK INDEX PARTNUM
SELECT SECONDARY
```

```
USE SUPPLIER
IF .NOT. FILE('SHORTNME.NDX')
  INDEX ON SHORT TO SHORTNME
ENDIF
USE SUPPLIER INDEX SHORTNME
SELECT PRIMARY
STORE 0 TO COUNTER
STORE 1 TO LINE
ERASE
@ 5,5 SAY 'SET PRINTER TO TOP OF PAGE'
@ 7,5 SAY 'PRESS RETURN TO CONTINUE'
WAIT
SET FORMAT TO PRINT
@ 1,30 SAY 'REORDER REPORT'
DO WHILE .NOT. EOF
  STORE REORDER – (ON:HAND + ON:ORDER) TO NUM
  IF NUM > 0
    STORE LINE + 3 TO LINE
    @ LINE,1 SAY PART:NO
    @ LINE,10 SAY DESCRIPT
    @ LINE,20 SAY COMPUTER
    STORE LINE + 1 TO LINE
    @ LINE,5 SAY 'REORDER'
    @ LINE,13 SAY NUM USING '9999'
    @ LINE,18 SAY '@'
    @ LINE,20 SAY COST USING '9999.99'
    @ LINE,28 SAY 'TOTAL'
    @ LINE,34 SAY COST * NUM USING '999,999.99'
    STORE TRIM(SUPPLIER) TO KEY
    SELECT SECONDARY
    FIND &KEY
```

```
      IF # <> 0
        STORE LINE + 1 TO LINE
        @ LINE,1 SAY FULL
        STORE LINE + 1 TO LINE
        @ LINE,1 SAY ADR
        @ LINE,30 SAY CITY
      ELSE
        STORE LINE + 1 TO LINE
        @ LINE,5 SAY KEY + ' NOT FOUND'
      ENDIF # <> 0
      STORE COUNTER + 1 TO COUNTER
      IF COUNTER = 9
        EJECT
        @ 1,30 SAY 'REORDER REPORT'
        STORE 0 TO COUNTER
        STORE 1 TO LINE
      ENDIF COUNTER = 9
      SELECT PRIMARY
    ENDIF NUM > 0
    SKIP
  ENDDO WHILE .NOT. EOF
  EJECT
  SET FORMAT TO SCREEN
  RELEASE ALL EXCEPT CHOICE
  RETURN
```

First, the two files required are USEd as usual. Then we SELECT PRIMARY, the STOCK database. We then put a 0 in COUNTER, which is used to keep track of where we are on the printed page.

We want the report to go to the printer, so we SET FORMAT TO PRINT. LINE is used to select the line to be printed on.

The WHILE loop runs through the whole STOCK database, record by record. We use NUM to contain the number of items to reorder and to see whether the total of the items on hand and on order does or does not equal the reorder level.

If NUM is greater than 0, we need to reorder. We print the part number, description, and computer on the first line. The second line tells how many items to reorder, the individual cost, and the total cost.

We then get the short name from STOCK, switch to the secondary database SUPPLIER, and try to FIND the supplier data. If the supplier data is found, (that is, if # <> 0), we print the supplier name on the next line, and then the address. If we can't find the supplier, then we print NOT FOUND.

Next we increment (add 1 to) the COUNTER, and if its value reaches nine, we start a new page of printout.

We then switch back to the primary database STOCK, SKIP to the next record, and do it all again.

When the report has been completed, we SET FORMAT TO SCREEN, RELEASE most of the memory variables, and RETURN to the menu.

Notice that $ symbols were not used for the @ rows. Some printers (for example, the EPSON FX-80) produce form feeds instead of line feeds in response to the $. The variable LINE can be used instead.

You might wish to change the format of the report presented here. Notice that there is no automatic update of the ON ORDER quantity in STOCK. This can be done by the operator when the order is actually placed. If you would prefer automatic updating, feel free to change the program. It requires only one additional line.

MAKING CHANGES TO THE PROGRAM

There are several changes you might wish to make in the program. For example, you might wish to combine the search, change, and delete functions into one. If you do this, provide a submenu to call the three. Use the USE statement once only; that way you won't lose your place in the file when you switch among the three functions. You'll have to combine the three in the main menu, too, and have the main menu call the submenu. This should be an easy change to make, and making it will give you some practice. Try it.

Another change might be to add some easy ways to cancel a menu choice, in case the operator made the wrong menu choice or changed his or her mind after starting to use a function.

The code for this program was put in the order so that would make the files easiest to understand. But to make the command files shorter, you might put some of the statement groups that are common to several files in a single command file and call them as required. Examples are the lists of STOREs and REPLACEs.

Rather than checking for an index file for each menu choice, you might do this for both files at the beginning of the menu file. This would save some time. Then USE the indexed files without the check in each called command file.

Remember, these files were written to be easy to understand; they are not necessarily the best, most compact, and most efficient files that could be written! See how you can improve them with the hints already given. It will be good practice.

ENTERING DATA

To use the program, type

DO MENU

Select A from the menu for ADD NEW STOCK, and type in the data supplied on page 124. After you've finished these entries, choose F for ADD NEW SUP-PLIER and type in the supplier data on pages 125 and 126.

Work with the program to get the user's perspective on how all the command files work.

Chapter 9

_____Quickcode_____

As mentioned in the introduction, Quickcode is a popular program generator designed to be used with dBASE II. It can quickly and easily create a single database file. This chapter gives a quick description of how the program works. Then, in Chapter 10, we'll use Quickcode to reproduce the inventory program we wrote in Chapter 8.

Quickcode will produce all the standard command files required to use a database. First you must design the structure. As you do when you design a database by hand, you select the width, type, and number of decimal places. One limitation is that you can use only integers (no decimal point), numbers with one decimal place, and numbers with two decimal places. If you need more than two, you're out of luck. Another limitation is that you cannot have a database that refers to another database, as in the REORDER command file in Chapter 8's inventory program. However, you can overcome such limitations by changing Quickcode's generated command files or add your own command files to the menu, as we'll see in Chapter 10.

All the usual command files are produced from your structure, including a menu and files to add a record, delete a record, search for a record, edit a record, print a record, and print a report.

You can easily add automatic error checking when you set up the structure, setting minimum and maximum legal values or checks against a list or file of legal entries. You can have indexed files, with several indexes if you wish.

Besides character, numeric, and logical fields, you can have subsets of these types; for example, integer, numeric with one decimal place, numeric with two decimal places, social security numbers, dates, and telephone numbers.

You can set up the screen display any way you wish, including display only text, rather than text prompts requiring data together. You can also design and print labels from your database.

When you use the report function, you must fill out dBASE II's report form, just as you've done before. Quickcode does not design the report format. The first time you select a report printout from the menu you will automatically be switched to dBASE II's report module to create the report structure. You can set up several report formats for the same database if you wish. You can use the subtotal feature, too, if the file is indexed to take advantage of it. Review Chapter 5 for more details.

INSTALLATION

Don't forget to make a backup of your Quickcode diskette(s) before you try to run the program. If you are using the IBM PC system you won't need to install the program; that is already done for you.

As with dBASE II, if you're installing the program in another system, you usually need only select your system from the menu. If it's not on the menu, you'll have to go through a custom installation question-and-answer session. If this is the case, you might need some help from your dealer.

The command to make an installation is QINSTALL. Simply type this from your operating system prompt (probably A>), and follow the directions. The Quickcode manual gives all the details. It shouldn't take you more than a few minutes to make the installation and test it.

With a system using CP/M, if you're using Quickcode from a backup, as you should be, you next copy the CP/M operating system to the diskette. The name of the command to use varies with the CP/M card and the implementation you are using.

If you are using PC-DOS or MS-DOS, you should have transferred the operating system when you formatted the diskette. Then use

```
A> COPY *.* B:
```

to copy the Quickcode diskette from drive A to drive B, for example.

You can put your Quickcode files on hard disk if you have one.

You are now ready to run Quickcode.

Note: The Apple version (and perhaps others) requires you to use two diskettes to run Quickcode. The program will prompt you to change diskettes when necessary.

STARTING QUICKCODE

Enter

```
A> qc
```

First you get the Quickcode copyright notice; then the main menu is displayed (Fig. 9-1).

```
                    QUICKCODE: HELP FOR THE WEARY USER
---------------------------------------------------------------------------
SCREEN EDITING COMMANDS                              OTHER COMMANDS
---------------------------------------------------------------------------
CMD      ENTER ! CMD      ENTER ! CMD      ENTER ! CMD     ENTER ! CMD     ENTER
---------------------------------------------------------------------------
RIGHT    CTRL-D! LINE     CTRL-L! GRID     CTRL-G! HELP       ?! FIELDS   CTRL-B
LEFT     CTRL-S! COLUMN   CTRL-C! TOGGLE   CTRL-Z! SAVE    CTRL-P!
UP       CTRL-E! DEL LINE CTRL-F! CAR RTN RETURN! EXIT       ESC!
DOWN     CTRL-X! DEL COL  CTRL-V!                !  *QUIT  CTRL-_!
MIDDLE   CTRL-Y! CENTER   CTRL-O!                !
LMARGIN  CTRL-T! LSHIFT   CTRL-Q!                !
RMARGIN  CTRL-U! RSHIFT   CTRL-W!                !
TAB        TAB! *ERASE    CTRL-J!                !
------------ COMMANDS YOU CAN TYPE NOW ----------------------------------
CMD   WHAT IT DOES:        CMD    WHAT IT DOES:     !   PROGRAMS TO GENERATE
C     CONFIGURE SYSTEM      O     OLD SCREEN        !
S     SCREEN CHARACT.       N     NEW SCREEN        !ADD    GET    OUT   SCR
X     OUTPUT OPTIONS        T     LOAD TEXT FILE    !PRG    GO     RPT   DEF
M     QUICKMENU            ESC    GENERATE PGMS --->!ED     IO     VAL   PRN
                            G     GENERATE ONE PGM  !FAU
Q   ** QUICKSCREEN MODE     E     *** EXIT ***      !
---CURRENT SCREEN IS  NONAME     (AUTO PILOT ON)----------------------------
                 ENTER COMMAND
```

Fig. 9-1. The Quickcode main menu.

In the top portion of the menu you'll see a list of commands followed by their command codes. Remember, the ^ stands for the control key <Ctrl>; hold down <Ctrl> as you press the character following the ^ Esc means press the Escape key.

EDITING COMMANDS

The Quickcode editing commands used on the IBM PC are as follows (commands vary a little with different versions of Quickcode):

Command	Keys	Description
RIGHT	^D	Move cursor one space right.
LEFT	^S	Move cursor one space left.
UP	^E	Move cursor up one line.
DOWN	^X	Move cursor down one line.

Command	Keys	Description
MIDDLE	^Y	Move cursor to center of line.
LMARGIN	^T	Move cursor to left margin.
RMARGIN	^U	Move cursor to right margin.
TAB	TAB key	Move cursor to next tab stop.
LINE	^L	Draw a line to the right of the cursor. Character following code is used.
COLUMN	^C	Draw a vertical line down from the cursor. Character following code is used.
DEL LIN	^F	Delete all to right of cursor on line.
DEL COL	^V	Delete all of column below cursor.
CENTER	^O	Center text on line.
LSHIFT	^Q	Shift the line to the right of the cursor one space to the left.
RSHIFT	^W	Shift the line to the left of the cursor one space to the right.
ERASE	^]	Erase contents of screen.
GRID	^G	Puts an alignment grid on the screen, or if it's already there, removes the grid.

You should experiment, using these commands with Quickcode until you are familiar with their effects.

OTHER COMMANDS
WITHIN QUICKCODE

Other important commands you can use from within Quickcode are these:

Command	Keys	Description
HELP	?	Returns to main menu.
SAVE	^P	Saves your screen description file to disk. Normally, use EXIT instead, unless you haven't finished the screen design. Once the screen design is completed and you've used the Esc key to generate the program files, the screen description is saved as well. So if you need to leave Quickcode and haven't finished generating your programs, use SAVE to save what you have.

Command	Keys	Description
GENERATE PROGRAMS	Esc key	Leave Quickscreen (screen generation mode) and generate all the command files.
QUIT	^_	Leave Quickcode and go to the operating system. If SAVE or Esc was not used, using Quit causes loss of your screen description.
FIELDS	^B	Go to fields mode to set up details of database structure.

CHANGING THE QUICKCODE COMMANDS

Changing the Quickcode editing and other codes is possible but not advisable; try the Quickcode default codes for a while first. If you want to change any of the editing or other command codes, start by typing C (configuration menu) when in the main menu. You can then alter any of the codes. See the Quickcode manual for details on changing codes. Watch out for duplication!

OTHER COMMANDS USED FROM THE MAIN MENU

Command	Definition
O	Call up an old screen description file.
N	Change the name of the present screen description. You must then use ^P (SAVE) or Esc (GENERATE PROGRAMS) to save the screen description under that new name.
T	Read in a text file.
E	Exit Quickcode. Be sure to SAVE (^P) your screen description first.
C	Go to configuration menu.
S	Go to screen description menu; details later.
X	Go to the output options menu. This will permit you to select the command files to generate; details later.
M	Go to Quickmenu to generate a custom menu.
Esc	Generate command files. Same as exit command.
Q	Go to Quickscreen mode, where you can lay out the screen and supply the database structure (by means of ^B).

SETTING UP A SAMPLE DATABASE

For the first example of using Quickcode, let's generate the command files required to use our old ZOO database.

This description of Quickcode operation will hit the high points. Following the procedure described here will help you learn how to set up a database quickly. If you need more details, see Chapter 10 and read the Quickcode manual.

Leave the Auto Pilot function on.

First type N, then rename the screen (presently NONAME) to ZOO.

Now type Q from the main menu to get to Quickscreen.

Screen Format

Next use the editing commands to set up a screen format. You can use the simple example shown here, (see also Fig. 9-2).

ZOO INVENTORY

ANIMAL	;ANIMAL
QUANTITY	;QUANTITY#
DATE	;DATE
CAGE NUMBER	;CAGE:NO#
SEX	;SEX
VALUE	;VALUE$

The names to the left are the names used for prompts. The names to the right are the field variable names. These must begin with a semicolon and follow the rules for dBASE II field variable names outlined in Chapter 3. Additionally, for Quickcode these names can be no more than 9 characters long (dBASE II allows 10). You also need to add a $ to the end of the name if the value is to have one or two decimal places, or a # if the value is to be an integer. These special characters are not included in the field name and do not count as one of the 9 characters allowed; nor does the semicolon.

When you created your screen, you probably didn't much care for the editing features. The arrow keys and the Backspace key didn't work as expected. And it's hard to get used to using control characters. Have patience; you'll get used to the editor after a while, and then it won't be so hard to use.

When the screen is displayed, the prompts will be shown as on the screen example in Fig. 9-2. The data will be entered beginning at the position of the semicolon in front of the field variable name. You could put the field variable name under the prompt and enter your data there if you wish (see Fig. 9-3).

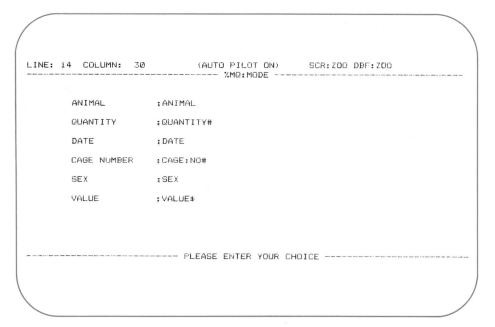

Fig. 9-2. A Screen format for ZOO.

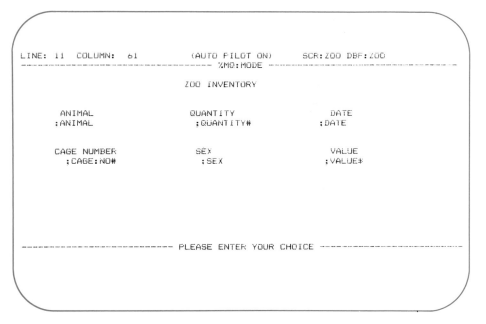

Fig. 9-3. An Alternate screen format for ZOO.

The title ZOO INVENTORY and the prompts are not tied to the field variable names in any way. They are just displayed at the positions shown on the screen when data is entered.

The number sign (#) following the field name indicates that it is a numeric field, with an integer value. The dollar sign denotes that the variable can contain a value with one or two decimal places. Remember, Quickcode permits no more than two decimal places (unfortunately). Unmarked field names are of character type.

You can have up to 22 prompts, titles, and field variable names on one line. You can have up to 64 prompts, titles, and field variable names (only 32 can be field variable names) on one screen. Once again, field variable names are limited to a maximum length of nine characters, not including the semicolon or special terminating character, such as the # or $.

Record Structure

Once you have laid out the screen as you wish, type ^B to go to the Fields mode (see Fig. 9-4).

The LEN values may be different in your display, depending on where you put the field variables when you set up your screen. If we let Quickscreen generate the files now, the lengths (LEN) and types (T) shown in Fig. 9-4 would be the result. Obviously, the long lengths of the character and numeric fields would waste a lot of disk space.

```
 #  FIELD NAME  T LEN F DEFAULT     MINIMUM     MAXIMUM     ERROR MESSAGE   VAL   ER
 0  MQ:MODE     C 7     *NONE*      *NONE*      *NONE*      *NONE*           *     3
 1  ANIMAL      C 55  F *NONE*      *NONE*      *NONE*      *NONE*           *     0
 2  QUANTITY    I 11  F *NONE*      *NONE*      *NONE*      *NONE*           *     0
 3  DATE        C 55  F *NONE*      *NONE*      *NONE*      *NONE*           *     0
 4  CAGE:NO     I 11  F *NONE*      *NONE*      *NONE*      *NONE*           *     0
 5  SEX         C 55  F *NONE*      *NONE*      *NONE*      *NONE*           *     0
 6  VALUE       $ 11  F *NONE*      *NONE*      *NONE*      *NONE*           *     0
```

Fig. 9-4. The Fields screen before changes.

So let's do a little editing. We'll use the screen editing codes to edit the fields data. We'll take the columns one at a time.

The first is the # column. This is simply the field variable number, generated in sequence, as Quickcode found each field variable on the screen (remember the semicolon indicator?).

The second is the type column. We see

C   Character

I   Integer (no decimal places)

$ Money (two decimal places)

We can change to

N   Numeric (one decimal place)   from $

D   Date   from   C

T   Telephone   from   C

S   Social security number   from   C

L   Logical   from   C

We'll change the Date type from C to D and leave the others as they are.

The next column is the length (width) of the data. Following our old ZOO structure, we'll set them this way:

ANIMAL   20

QUANTITY   3

DATE   8

CAGE:NO   3

SEX   1

VALUE   7

Note that you need to press the RETURN key after each length entry.

The next column is the file status (F). The possibilities are

F   File field (a Quickcode screen field that will appear in the database)

0–9   Key field (a field to be used for indexing)

Space   Nondatabase field (a field that will not become part of the database)

We'll leave all but ANIMAL set to F. Set ANIMAL to 0. This means it is our primary key (index). If we wanted to set secondary indexes, we'd number them 1 through 9, the most important first.

The next column is for the defaults. The values are set to whatever is in this column before it is changed by a STORE or GET. We'll set QUANTITY, CAGE:NO, and VALUE to 0, and DATE to 000000 (Quickcode will change it to 00/00/00). The others we'll leave alone.

The next column is MINIMUM. This represents the smallest value that will be accepted. To avoid negative number entry, we'll set QUANTITY, CAGE:NO, and VALUE to 0 in this column.

The next column is MAXIMUM. This is the largest value that will be accepted when data is entered. We'll leave all these set to *NONE*.

The next column is ERROR MESSAGE. This is the message that would be displayed when the data entry is less than the MINIMUM or greater than the MAXIMUM. We'll leave these set to *NONE* also.

Validating Entries

The next column is VALIDATION METHOD. This is used to indicate the type of validation to be used. Possibilities are

*	Minimum/maximum
L or N	List checking
F	File checking

This is a complex feature. See the Quickcode manual for an explanation. For our purposes now, leave them set to *.

The last column is for the ERROR CODE. This is set by Quickcode and must be 0 or 3. If you see another number, you have a problem. The codes are

0	No error
1	Name too long (maximum 9 characters)
2	Illegal character in field name
3	Display-only field (no error)
4	Too many fields (maximum thirty-two)
5	Duplicated field name

Use the editing code control keys to move around the Fields display to make your changes. To get back to the main menu (perhaps to check an editing code) use ?; Q and ^B will then get you back to the Fields display. (Your version of Quickcode may use a different command.)

After you've made the suggested changes, you should see something similar to Fig. 9-5. Now use ? to get back to the main menu.

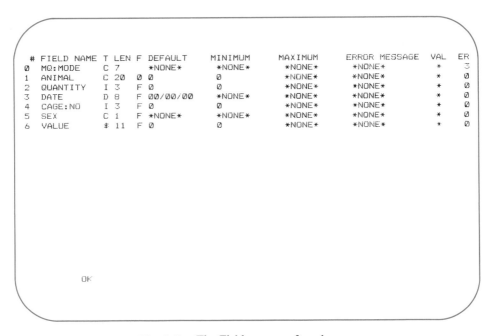

```
  # FIELD NAME  T LEN F DEFAULT     MINIMUM     MAXIMUM     ERROR MESSAGE   VAL  ER
  0 MO:MODE     C 7     *NONE*      *NONE*      *NONE*      *NONE*           *   3
  1 ANIMAL      C 20  0 0           0           *NONE*      *NONE*           *   0
  2 QUANTITY    I 3   F 0           0           *NONE*      *NONE*           *   0
  3 DATE        D 8   F 00/00/00    *NONE*      *NONE*      *NONE*           *   0
  4 CAGE:NO     I 3   F 0           0           *NONE*      *NONE*           *   0
  5 SEX         C 1   F *NONE*      *NONE*      *NONE*      *NONE*           *   0
  6 VALUE       $ 11  F 0           0           *NONE*      *NONE*           *   0




          OK
```

Fig. 9-5.   The Fields screen after changes.

CHOOSING COMMAND FILES
TO GENERATE

Type X from the main menu to enter the PROGRAMS GENERATED MENU (see Fig. 9-6). This is easy to use; just be sure you end up with a Y after the files you wish to generate and an N after the files you don't wish to generate. Normally, the files to be turned off (N) are files 9 and 15; the others should be left on. *Never turn off file 13!* (These file numbers may be different if you are using a different version of Quickcode. Check your Quickcode manual.)

To exit, use S first if you wish to make this the default file list (not a bad idea). Then use E to return to the main menu. See the bottom line of the screen for the codes.

When you get back to the main menu, look down at the lower right corner of the screen. You'll see the files there that you selected to be written by Quickcode.

If you should wish to make mailing labels, leave file 9 set to Y.

Now use the Escape key to generate the command files. Be sure you have room

```
                =  QUICKCODE PROGRAMS GENERATED  =

  PROGRAM                       OUTPUT?
  -------------------------------------------------------------

  (1)   ADD TO FILE (.ADD)       Y
  (2)   MAIN (.PRG)              Y
  (3)   DATABASE FILE (.DBF)     Y
  (4)   EDIT FILE (.ED)          Y
  (5)   SET DEFAULTS (.FAU)      Y
  (6)   GET FROM FILE (.GET)     Y
  (7)   SET UP FILE (.GO)        Y
  (8)   I/O SCREEN (.IO)         Y
  (9)   LABELS/FORMS (.LBL)      N
  (10)  OUTPUT SCREEN (.OUT)     Y
  (11)  SCREEN IMAGE (.PRN)      Y
  (12)  RUN REPORT (.RPT)        Y
  (13)  SCREEN DEFINITION (.SCR) Y
  (14)  VALIDATE ENTRY (.VAL)    Y
  (15)  WordStar (.WS)           N

  -------------------------------------------------------------
             ( S = SAVE.  E = EXIT.  Q = QUICKSCREEN MODE )
  ENTER # TO CHANGE:
```

Fig. 9-6. The Quickcode X menu.

on your diskette for all the generated files! Normally, you should have room for 15 filenames in the directory, with 30K to 40K of disk space remaining. But as long as you save the .SCR file (it will go on the diskette first), you can always generate the command files again if you want to alter the Quickcode screen — for example, to correct a spelling error. You must have this .SCR file, as it contains your screen description and the Fields data. Your dBASE II program files must also be on this diskette.

THE DEFAULT DRIVE

To put your Quickcode statements and the dBASE II files (except for the .PRG file) and your database file on a drive other than the one you are using for Quickcode, go to the S menu from the main menu (type S), and change the DEFAULT DRIVE (22) from ** to the desired drive — B:, C:, and so on (see Fig. 9-7). Then be sure you have a formatted (initialized) diskette in that drive before you use Esc to generate the command files and dBASE II file. (Your version of Quickcode may be different; again, check the Quickcode manual.)

From now on, the command file diskette will have to be in this drive, or the operating system won't be able to find the files. You can't change this default after the files are generated. You'd have to go back to the S menu and change the default drive setting back to **, then go to the main menu and generate the files again. You can also prefix the filename with the drive letter.

```
                          QUICKCODE
                   = SCREEN CHARACTERISTICS =
--------------------------------------------------------------------
  (1)   START OF DISPLAY FIELD            %   (18) ALT .OUT NAME      ZOO
  (2)   START OF DATABASE FIELD           :   (19) ALT .LBL NAME      ZOO
  (3)   END OF FIELD                      >   (20) LABEL SIZE         35
  (4)   HORIZONTAL LINE CHARACTER         -   (21) UNIQUE KEY         N
  (5)   VERTICAL COLUMN CHARACTER         !   (22) DEFAULT DRIVE      **
  (6)   LINE/COLUMN INTERSECT CHARACTER   +
  (7)   LEFT MARGIN    (MIN=0)            0
  (8)   RIGHT MARGIN   (MAX=131)          79
  (9)   TOP MARGIN     (MIN=0)            1
  (10)  BOTTOM MARGIN  (MAX=23)           20
  (11)  QUICKMENU CHARACTER               )
  (12)  DATABASE NAME                     ZOO
  (13)  AUTOMATIC PILOT                   Y
  (14)  LINE/COLUMN MONITOR               Y
  (15)  dBASE-II VERSION 2.3              Y
  (16)  TAB SIZE                          4
  (17)  TOP LINE NUMBER                   0
--------------------------------------------------------------------
                ( S = SAVE, E = EXIT, Q = QUICKSCREEN MODE )
  ENTER # TO CHANGE:
```

Fig. 9-7.   The Quickcode S menu.

RECOVERING YOUR
OLD ZOO DATABASE

This is as simple as it can be. When Quickcode is generating the command files, it will discover your old ZOO.DBF database file. It will ask if you want to retain this file. Simply tell it yes.

WORKING WITH YOUR ZOO PROGRAM

Type in

. do zoo

to dBASE II. You should now see a menu with your choices (Fig. 9-8). Let's examine them one at a time.

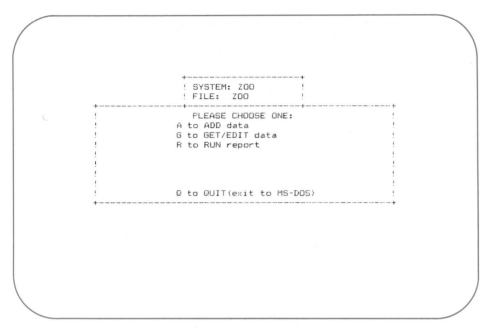

```
                    +-----------------------+
                    ! SYSTEM: ZOO          !
                    ! FILE:   ZOO          !
         +----------+-----------------------+----------------+
         !              PLEASE CHOOSE ONE:                   !
         !          A to ADD data                            !
         !          G to GET/EDIT data                       !
         !          R to RUN report                          !
         !                                                   !
         !                                                   !
         !                                                   !
         !          Q to QUIT(exit to MS-DOS)                !
         +---------------------------------------------------+
```

Fig. 9-8.   A Quickcode-generated program main menu.

Adding Records

The A choice lets you add new animals to the ZOO database (Fig. 9-9). The data is entered between the colons. The type of data must be correct. Try putting a negative number in a numeric field (remember the 0 MINIMUMs we set?). Try putting letters in a numeric field. You must press the RETURN key after entering each field's data. When you leave the last field, you'll get a new screen. Leave the first field (ANIMAL) blank and press ^W to stop entering new animals, or just reply with the RETURN key to all the fields. This method is the same as that used when entering data manually with dBASE II.

Looking at Records

Use G to look at records. Notice the new menu at the bottom of the screen (see Fig. 9-10).

N   Next record

P   Previous record

S   Search for record

M   Delete, edit, or print record

```
---------------------------------------- ADD ----------------------------------------
                              ZOO INVENTORY

   ANIMAL          :                         :
   QUANTITY        :  0:
   DATE            :00/00/00:
   CAGE NUMBER     :  0:
   SEX             : :
   VALUE           :   0.00:










          MAKE AS MANY ENTRIES AS YOU WANT
          WHEN DONE ENTER BLANKS FOR ANIMAL
```

Fig. 9-9.   A Quickcode-generated ADD menu.

```
---------------------------------------- GET ----------------------------------------
                              ZOO INVENTORY

   ANIMAL          ant
   QUANTITY          2
   DATE            01/12/84
   CAGE NUMBER      10
   SEX             f
   VALUE              0.03










          ENTER N FOR NEXT, P FOR PREVIOUS
             S FOR SEARCH, M FOR MORE COMMANDS
          PRESS RETURN WHEN DONE: :
```

Fig. 9-10.   A Quickcode-generated GET menu.

The N and P choices are self-explanatory. When you enter S, you'll be asked for a value to search for. Since we have only one key field, ANIMAL, only that data can be entered. Later on in this chapter, dSCAN will be discussed. It permits more detailed searches and relational searches.

When you enter an animal, the first record with that animal will appear. If there are other records with the same animal name, you can use N to get the next one. Be sure to use the correct case! If you put in tiger, you won't find TIGER.

Once you've found the record you want, you can use M (more) to edit, print, or delete it.

Try E. You just overtype any of the fields you wish to change. If the replacement entry has fewer characters than the original field, use the space bar to type blank spaces over the remaining characters. Press <ENTER> when you have completed the replacement entry. When you have finished, answer "ANY MORE CHANGES?" with an N.

To delete a record, type a D, then a Y in answer to the "ARE YOU SURE?" question.

To delete the records permanently (PACK), answer that question with a Y.

To print a record (just that one record), type P, and then follow the instructions.

Reports

To print a report, select that function from the menu. Then, if your response to the report filename question asks for a report form that was never used, you'll have to fill in the usual dBASE II report question and answer form. You can set up several report forms for the same database; just give each a different name. Instead of immediately printing the report, you can send the report file to a disk file.

dSCAN

If you wish to do a more elaborate search than was permitted by the earlier search routine, use dSCAN. This is a simplified version of the SEARCH command file we used in Chapter 8.

Whenever you might wish to use dSCAN, the program will give you that opportunity by making dSCAN available on the menu.

If you select dSCAN in the menu, you must actually enter data when asked, or enter T or TRUE if you change your mind. If you press the RETURN key without entering data, T, or TRUE, terrible things may happen (says the manual). The dSCAN selection criterion uses the field names, *not* the prompts. For example, use CAGE:NO, not CAGE NUMBER.

You learned about relational searches starting in Chapter 4, when the LOCATE command was discussed. An example of using dSCAN would be to enter the criterion

SEX = 'f'

or the criteria

SEX = 'f' .AND. VALUE > 100

or any other combination of the relational commands you learned earlier. The main things to watch out for are using the correct field names, putting strings in delimiters, and using parentheses where necessary. Don't forget the periods around AND and OR.

SUMMING UP

You now know how to create a simple database program. See how simple it was? Much easier to let Quickcode write the command files if the program is a simple one. It lives up to its name too: it's very quick! In the next chapter, we'll let Quickcode do its version of the inventory program we wrote in Chapter 8.

Chapter 10

___Putting Quickcode to Work___

In this chapter we'll use Quickcode to reproduce the software inventory program written in Chapter 8.

You already know the essentials of using Quickcode. Remember all the typing you had to do to enter all those command files in Chapter 8? Now watch how simple Quickcode makes it.

Enter Quickcode and use N to rename the file. Call it STOCK. Next use Q and set up your screen. Here are the prompts and field names we used in Chapter 8.

Prompt	Field name
PART NO	PART:NO
DESCRIPTION	DESCRIPT
ON HAND	ON:HAND#
REORDER	REORDER#
PRICE	PRICE$
COST	COST$
SUPPLIER	SUPPLIER
COMPUTER	COMPUTER
ON ORDER	ON:ORDER#

Set up the screen in any way you like. One choice is shown in Fig. 10-1. Next use ^B to get to the Fields screen. The structure we used in Chapter 8 was

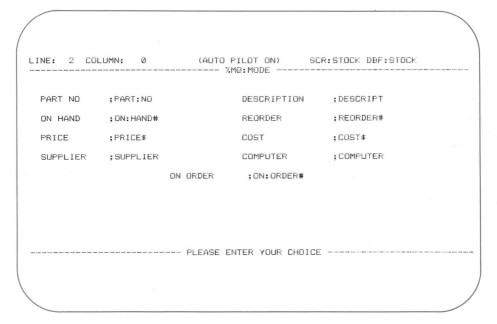

Fig. 10-1. A screen format for STOCK.

PART:NO,C,8

DESCRIPT,C,9

ON:HAND,I,4

REORDER,I,4

PRICE,$,7

COST,$,7

SUPPLIER,C,9

COMPUTER,C,9

ON:ORDER,I,4

Index on the part number field by using a 0 in the F field.

Use whatever defaults, error messages, and so on, you wish. When you've finished, use ^B to get back to Quickscreen, then ? to return to the main menu. See Fig. 10-2 for some choices.

You may use the X menu to be sure the correct files will be generated, and perhaps the S menu to use another disk drive for the generated files.

```
     #  FIELD NAME  T  LEN  F  DEFAULT    MINIMUM    MAXIMUM    ERROR MESSAGE    VAL    ER
     Ø  MQ:MODE     C  7       *NONE*     *NONE*     *NONE*     *NONE*           *      3
     1  PART:NO     C  8    Ø  *NONE*     *NONE*     *NONE*     *NONE*           *      Ø
     2  DESCRIPT    C  9    F  *NONE*     *NONE*     *NONE*     *NONE*           *      Ø
     3  ON:HAND     I  4    F  Ø          Ø          *NONE*     *NONE*           *      Ø
     4  REORDER     I  4    F  Ø          Ø          *NONE*     *NONE*           *      Ø
     5  PRICE       $  7    F  Ø          Ø          *NONE*     *NONE*           *      Ø
     6  COST        $  7    F  Ø          Ø          *NONE*     *NONE*           *      Ø
     7  SUPPLIER    C  9    F  *NONE*     *NONE*     *NONE*     *NONE*           *      Ø
     8  COMPUTER    C  9    F  *NONE*     *NONE*     *NONE*     *NONE*           *      Ø
     9  ON:ORDER    I  4    F  Ø          Ø          *NONE*     *NONE*           *      Ø
```

Fig. 10-2. A Fields screen for STOCK after changes.

Now use the Esc key to generate the files. As happened when you generated the ZOO files in Chapter 8, when Quickcode attempts to generate the STOCK.DBF file, it will find your old one. Just tell Quickcode to leave the old database file alone; then you won't have to load all the data again. There, you've finished one-third of the task already!

Now use N from the main menu to change the name to SUPPLIER. Use Q to return to Quickscreen. You can erase the old STOCK screen with ^]. Now set up the SUPPLIER screen. The prompts and field names we used in Chapter 8 were

Prompt	Field name
SHORT NAME	SHORT
FULL NAME	FULL
ADDRESS	ADR
CITY STATE ZIP	CITY

Now use ^B to get to the Fields mode. The structure we used for SUPPLIER in Chapter 8 was

SHORT,C,10

FULL,C,20

ADR,C,25

CITY,C,24

You probably won't need to set up any defaults for this screen. Use a 0 in the F field to index on SHORT.

Now use the Escape key to generate the SUPPLIER files. Now you've finished two-thirds of the job!

A NEW MENU

Next we'll generate a master menu to call the STOCK and SUPPLIER menus. We'll call the new menu SOFTWARE.

The DOS was used to copy the STOCK.PRG file to SOFTWARE.PRG. Then dBASE II's MODIFY COMMAND SOFTWARE was used to edit it to look like the following. If you wish, you can simply write the following file from scratch.

```
SET TALK OFF

SET FORMAT TO SCREEN

DO WHILE T

 ERASE

@ 5,27 SAY ' + -------------------- +'

@ 6,27 SAY '! MAIN :'

@ 6,37 SAY 'MENU'

@ 6,48 SAY '!'

@ 7,27 SAY '!'

@ 7,48 SAY '!'

@ 8,11 SAY ' + --------------- + -------------------- + ---------------- +'

@ 9,11 SAY '!                    PLEASE CHOOSE ONE:'

@ 9,64 SAY '!'

@ 10,11 SAY '!'

@ 10,26 SAY 'A to use STOCK database'

@ 10,64 SAY '!'
```

```
@ 11,11 SAY '!'
@ 11,26 SAY 'B to use SUPPLIER database'
@ 11,64 SAY '!'
@ 12,11 SAY '!'
@ 12,26 SAY 'C to run REORDER report'
@ 12,64 SAY '!'
@ 13,11 SAY '!'
@ 13,64 SAY '!'
@ 14,11 SAY '!'
@ 14,64 SAY '!'
@ 15,11 SAY '!'
@ 15,64 SAY '!'
@ 16,11 SAY '!'
@ 16,64 SAY '!'
@ 17,11 SAY '!                    Q to QUIT (exit to MSDOS)'
@ 17,64 SAY '!'
@ 18,11 SAY ' + -------------------------------------------------- + '
@ 21,10 SAY '
SET CONSOLE OFF
WAIT TO CHOICE
SET CONSOLE ON
IF !(CHOICE) = 'A'
    DO STOCK
ELSE
  IF !(CHOICE) = 'B'
    DO SUPPLIER
ELSE
  IF !(CHOICE) = 'C'
    DO ORDER
ELSE
  IF !(CHOICE) = 'Q'
    QUIT
```

```
            ENDIF QUIT
            ENDIF ORDER
            ENDIF SUPPLIER
            ENDIF STOCK
        ENDDO
        RELEASE CHOICE
```

That's all there is to it. What we've done is combine the STOCK and SUPPLIER menus with the REORDER command file we wrote in Chapter 8. (We change its name from REORDER to ORDER a little later on.)

CHANGING FILES

The next step is to make some changes in the STOCK and SUPPLIER files. Complete files will not be printed here; only the changes will be shown. In the line at @ 17,11 SAY, change the

    Q to QUIT (exit to MSDOS)

to

    E to Exit to Main Menu

Change the

    IF ! (MQ:COMMAND) = 'Q'
        QUIT

to

    IF !(MQ:COMMAND) = 'E'
        RETURN

Make these changes in both the STOCK.PRG and SUPPLIER.PRG files.

Next we have to make a few slight changes in the REORDER command file. Leave Quickcode by using the exit option provided in the Quickcode menu. Then use your DOS to copy REORDER.PRG to ORDER.PRG. Next, make the following changes in ORDER.PRG. Use the dBASE II command

    . MODIFY COMMAND ORDER

In line 2 change PARTNUM.NDX to STOCK.NDX. In lines 3 and 5 change PARTNUM to STOCK. In line 8 change SHORTNME.NDX to SUPPLIER.NDX. In lines 9 and 11 change SHORTNME to SUPPLIER. That's it! This was done because Quickcode uses the database name for the index file name.

RUNNING THE PROGRAM

You can run this new combined program from dBASE II by using

. do software

And you can see how simple it is to create a fairly complex menu-driven database system with Quickcode.

MORE QUICKCODE

There are even more things Quickcode will do for you. You can read through the Quickcode manual to see the possibilities. However, you know enough now to create a database for most applications.

Be sure to consider your database file structure carefully. If you plan well, you can use the dBASE II REPORT function to create your reports quickly, saving a lot of manual programming.

The rest of this chapter is a listing of a set of typical Quickcode-generated command files. I used the ones Quickcode generated in Chapter 9 for the ZOO database. As you will see, these files are quite a bit like those written in Chapter 8.

Here is the .PRG file that calls all the other files. As you can see, it also provides the menu.

```
*    ZOO.PRG    -MAIN PROGRAM
* DATABASE NAME IS ZOO
* DATABASE IS KEYED
SET TALK OFF
SET FORMAT TO SCREEN
SELECT PRIMARY
STORE FILE('ZOO.NDX') TO MQ:NDX
IF .NOT. MQ:NDX
   DO ZOO.GO
   ERASE
```

```
     @ 21,10 SAY 'FILE IS NOW BEING INDEXED'
ENDIF
USE ZOO INDEX ZOO
STORE T TO MQ:MORE
DO WHILE MQ:MORE
   ERASE
@ 5,27 SAY '+ -------------------- +'
@ 6,27 SAY '! SYSTEM:'
@ 6,37 SAY 'ZOO'
@ 6,48 SAY '!'
@ 7,27 SAY '! FILE:'
@ 7,36 SAY 'ZOO'
@ 7,48 SAY '!'
@ 8,11 SAY '+ --------------- + -------------------- + --------------- +'
@ 9,11 SAY '!                    PLEASE CHOOSE ONE:'
@ 9,64 SAY '!'
@ 10,11 SAY '!'
@ 10,26 SAY 'A to ADD data'
@ 10,64 SAY '!'
@ 11,11 SAY '!'
@ 11,26 SAY 'G to GET/EDIT data'
@ 11,64 SAY '!'
@ 12,11 SAY '!'
@ 12,26 SAY 'R to RUN report'
@ 12,64 SAY '!'
@ 13,11 SAY '!'
@ 13,64 SAY '!'
@ 14,11 SAY '!'
@ 14,64 SAY '!'
@ 15,11 SAY '!'
@ 15,64 SAY '!'
```

```
@ 16,11 SAY '!'

@ 16,64 SAY '!'

@ 17,11 SAY '!                    Q to QUIT(exit to MSDOS)'

@ 17,64 SAY '!'

@ 18,11 SAY ' + -------------------------------------------------- +'

  @ 21,10 SAY '

  SET CONSOLE OFF

  WAIT TO MQ:COMMAND

  SET CONSOLE ON

  IF ! (MQ:COMMAND) = 'A'

    DO ZOO.ADD

  ELSE

  IF !(MQ:COMMAND) = 'G'

    DO ZOO.GET

ELSE

  IF !(MQ:COMMAND) = 'R'

    DO ZOO.RPT

ELSE

IF !(MQ:COMMAND) = 'Q'

    QUIT

    ENDIF QUIT

    ENDIF REPORT

    ENDIF GET

    ENDIF ADD

ENDDO

RELEASE MQ:MORE,MQ:COMMAND,MQ:NDX
```

Next is the ZOO.ADD file. As you would assume, this file is used to add records to the database. It calls the ZOO.FAU, ZOO.IO, and ZOO.VAL files. These will be listed later.

```
*     ZOO.ADD     -ADD PROGRAM

STORE T TO MQ:AMORE
DO WHILE MQ:AMORE
* SET UP DEFAULT VALUES
DO ZOO.FAU
ERASE
STORE 'ADD' TO MQ:MODE
* GET DATA TO ADD
DO ZOO.IO
@ 21,10 SAY 'MAKE AS MANY ENTRIES AS YOU WANT'
@ 22,10 SAY 'WHEN DONE ENTER BLANKS FOR ANIMAL'
READ
* ARE WE DONE?
IF MANIMAL<>'                    '
PERFORM VALIDATION
DO ZOO.VAL
APPEND BLANK
* PUT SCREEN DATA INTO FILE
REPLACE ANIMAL WITH MANIMAL
REPLACE QUANTITY WITH MQUANTITY
REPLACE DATE WITH MDATE
REPLACE CAGE:NO WITH MCAGE:NO
REPLACE SEX WITH MSEX
REPLACE VALUE WITH MVALUE
ELSE
    STORE F TO MQ:AMORE
ENDIF
ENDDO
RELEASE MQ:MODE,MQ:AMORE
```

```
* RELEASE INPUT FIELDS
RELEASE MANIMAL
RELEASE MQUANTITY
RELEASE MDATE
RELEASE MCAGE:NO
RELEASE MSEX
RELEASE MVALUE
```

Next is the ZOO.GET file, which is used to search, delete, print, and edit records. It calls the ZOO.ED and ZOO.OUT files.

```
* ZOO.GET    -GET PROGRAM
STORE ' T ' TO MQ:SLCT
STORE T TO MQ:GMORE
STORE 'N' TO MQ:GDEL
DO WHILE MQ:GMORE
ERASE
STORE ' GET ' TO MQ:MODE
* DISPLAY CURRENT RECORD
IF &MQ:SLCT
  DO ZOO.OUT
ENDIF
STORE ' ' TO MQ:CMD
@ 21,10 SAY 'ENTER N FOR NEXT, P FOR PREVIOUS'
@ 22,10 SAY '        S FOR SEARCH, M FOR MORE COMMANDS'
IF MQ:SLCT<> ' T '
    @ 23,4 SAY '**'
ENDIF
@ 23,10 SAY 'PRESS RETURN WHEN DONE' GET MQ:CMD
READ
IF !(MQ:CMD) = 'S'
STORE T TO MQ:SMORE
```

```
DO WHILE MQ:SMORE
  ERASE
  STORE ' SEARCH ' TO MQ:MODE
* GET FIELDS TO SEARCH FOR
@ 1,0 SAY '--------------------'
@ 1,20 SAY '--------------'
@ 1,44 SAY '--------------------'
@ 1,64 SAY '--------------'
@ 2,34 SAY 'ZOO INVENTORY'
@ 4,6 SAY 'ANIMAL'
STORE '                   ' TO MANIMAL
@ 4,22 GET MANIMAL
@ 5,6 SAY 'QUANTITY'
@ 6,6 SAY 'DATE'
@ 7,6 SAY 'CAGE NUMBER'
@ 8,6 SAY 'SEX'
@ 9,6 SAY 'VALUE'
  @ 21,10 SAY 'PLEASE ENTER VALUES TO SEARCH FOR '
  IF MQ:SLCT<> ' T '
  @ 23,4 SAY '**'
ENDIF
READ
* EXIT FROM LOOP IF FOUND
GOTO TOP
STORE TRIM(MANIMAL) TO MQ:KEY
IF MQ:SLCT = ' T '
FIND &MQ:KEY
IF # <> 0
    STORE F TO MQ:SMORE
ELSE
  @ 22,10 SAY 'NOT FOUND'
```

```
    @ 23,10 SAY 'TRY AGAIN (Y/N)?'
    SET CONSOLE OFF
    WAIT TO MQ:DUMMY
    SET CONSOLE ON
    IF !(MQ:DUMMY)<>'Y'
    STORE F TO MQ:SMORE
  ENDIF Y
  RELEASE MQ:DUMMY
    ENDIF # <> 0
  ELSE
    LOCATE FOR ANIMAL = MANIMAL .AND. &MQ:SLCT
    IF .NOT. EOF
      STORE F TO MQ:SMORE
  ELSE
    @ 22,10 SAY 'NOT FOUND'
    @ 23,10 SAY 'TRY AGAIN (Y/N)?'
    SET CONSOLE OFF
    WAIT TO MQ:DUMMY
    SET CONSOLE ON
    IF !(MQ:DUMMY)<>'Y'
    STORE F TO MQ:SMORE
  ENDIF Y
  RELEASE MQ:DUMMY
    ENDIF EOF
  ENDIF MQ:SLCT = T
ENDDO   MQ:SMORE
RELEASE MQ:SMORE
RELEASE MQ:KEY
ELSE
IF !(MQ:CMD) = 'N'
  STORE T TO MQ:N
```

```
    DO WHILE MQ:N
      SKIP
      IF &MQ:SLCT
      STORE F TO MQ:N
      ENDIF
      IF EOF
        STORE F TO MQ:N
        STORE ' T ' TO MQ:SLCT
        @ 23,4 SAY
      ENDIF
    ENDDO
    RELEASE MQ:N
  ELSE
  IF !(MQ:CMD) = 'P'
      STORE ' T ' TO MQ:SLCT
      @ 23,4 SAY '      '
      SKIP  − 1
  ELSE
    IF !(MQ:CMD) = 'M'
    STORE T TO MQ:MMORE
    DO WHILE MQ:MMORE
    STORE ' MORE ' TO MQ:MODE
    STORE '   ' TO MQ:MMD
    @ 21,10 SAY 'ENTER E TO EDIT, D TO DELETE,          '
    @ 22,10 SAY '       P TO PRINT, C TO dSCAN          '
    @ 23,0
    IF MQ:SLCT<> ' T '
      @ 23,4 SAY '**'
    ENDIF
    @ 23,10 SAY 'PRESS RETURN WHEN DONE '
    GET MQ:MMD
```

```
READ
IF !(MQ:MMD) = 'E'
    ERASE
IF MQ:SLCT <> ' T '
 @ 23,4 SAY '**'
ENDIF
* EDIT RECORD
  DO ZOO.ED
ELSE
IF !(MQ:MMD) = 'D'
    STORE 'N' TO MQ:ANS
 IF MQ:SLCT <> ' T '
  @ 23,4 SAY '**'
 ENDIF
@ 23,10 SAY 'ARE YOU SURE (Y/N)?                        '
@ 23,28 GET MQ:ANS
    READ
IF ! (MQ:ANS) = 'Y'
    DELETE
    STORE 'Y' TO MQ:GDEL
ENDIF
RELEASE MQ:ANS
ELSE
IF !(MQ:MMD) = 'P'
 @ 23,10 SAY 'PLEASE SET UP PRINTER
 STORE '     ' TO MQ:MODE
SET CONSOLE OFF
WAIT
SET CONSOLE ON
SET FORMAT TO PRINT
DO ZOO.OUT
```

```
    @ 25,0 SAY ' '
    SET FORMAT TO SCREEN
   ELSE
   IF !(MQ:MMD) = 'C'
    GOTO TOP
    STORE '
  ' TO MQ:SLCT
    @ 21,10 SAY 'PLEASE ENTER SELECTION CRITERIA
  '
    @ 22,10 SAY '     DO NOT PRESS RETURN!!!
  '
    @ 23,4 SAY '**'
    @ 23,10 GET MQ:SLCT
    READ
    LOCATE FOR &MQ:SLCT
    IF EOF
      @ 21,10 SAY 'NO MORE RECORDS CAN BE FOUND
  '
      @ 22,10 SAY 'PLEASE PRESS RETURN TO CONTINUE
  '
      @ 23,4 SAY ' '
      STORE ' T ' TO MQ:SLCT
      SET CONSOLE OFF
      WAIT
      SET CONSOLE ON
   ELSE
      DO ZOO.OUT
    ENDIF
   ELSE
    STORE F TO MQ:MMORE
  ENDIF F
```

```
ENDIF P

ENDIF D

ENDIF E

ENDDO MQ:MMORE

RELEASE MQ:MMORE,MQ:MMD

ELSE

    STORE F TO MQ:GMORE

ENDIF M

ENDIF P

ENDIF N

ENDIF S

ENDDO MQ:GMORE

IF MQ:GDEL = 'Y'

  STORE 'N' TO MQ:ANS

  @ 23,10 SAY 'WANT TO PERMANENTLY DELETE RECORDS(Y/N)'

  @ 23,49 GET MQ:ANS

  READ

  IF !(MQ:ANS) = 'Y'

    PACK

  ELSE

    RECALL ALL

  ENDIF

    RELEASE MQ:ANS

ENDIF MQ:GDEL

RELEASE MQ:CMD,MQ:GMORE,MQ:GDEL,MQ:SLCT

RELEASE MQ:MODE
```

The next file is the ZOO.RPT file.

```
*    ZOO.RPT-REPORT PROGRAM
```

```
* IF REPORT DOESN'T EXIST, GO INTO dBASE
```

```
STORE ' ' TO MQ:RLPT
DO WHILE !(MQ:RLPT) <> 'Y' .AND. !(MQ:RLPT) <> 'N'
STORE 'Y' TO MQ:RLPT
@ 21,10 SAY 'WANT REPORT SENT TO THE PRINTER?' GET MQ:RLPT
READ
ENDDO
  STORE ' ' TO MQ:RDSK
  DO WHILE !(MQ:RDSK) <> 'Y' .AND. !(MQ:RDSK) <> 'N'
  STORE 'N' TO MQ:RDSK
@ 21,10 SAY 'WANT REPORT SENT TO A FILE ?    ' GET MQ:RDSK
READ
ENDDO
IF !(MQ:RDSK) = 'Y'
STORE '           ' TO MQ:RFILE
DO WHILE MQ:RFILE = '        '
@ 22,10 SAY 'ENTER FILE NAME' GET MQ:RFILE
READ
ENDDO
STORE TRIM(MQ:RFILE) TO MQ:RFILE
ENDIF   RDSK
STORE '           ' TO MQ:RPT
  DO WHILE MQ:RPT = '    '
@ 23,10 SAY 'ENTER REPORT NAME' GET MQ:RPT
READ
ENDDO
IF !(MQ:RLPT) = 'Y'
@ 23,10 SAY 'PLEASE SET UP PRINTER        '
SET CONSOLE OFF
WAIT
SET CONSOLE ON
SET PRINT ON
ENDIF RLPT
IF !(MQ:RDSK) = 'Y'
```

```
SET ALTERNATE TO &MQ:RFILE
SET ALTERNATE ON
ENDIF RDSK
ERASE
REPORT FORM &MQ:RPT
SET PRINT OFF
SET ALTERNATE OFF
IF !(MQ:RDSK) = 'Y'
  RELEASE MQ:RDSK,MQ:RFILE
ENDIF
RELEASE MQ:RLPT, MQ:RPT
```

Next comes the ZOO.ED file, used by the ZOO.GET file for editing.

```
*    ZOO.ED    -EDIT PROGRAM
STORE T TO MQ:EMORE
 STORE ' EDIT ' TO MQ:MODE
* SET UP SCREEN VARIABLES
 STORE ANIMAL TO MANIMAL
 STORE QUANTITY TO MQUANTITY
 STORE DATE TO MDATE
 STORE CAGE:NO TO MCAGE:NO
 STORE SEX TO MSEX
 STORE VALUE TO MVALUE
DO WHILE MQ:EMORE
ERASE
* GET SCREEN INPUT
 DO ZOO.IO
 @ 21,10 SAY 'ENTER ALL CHANGES'
READ
* VALIDATE INPUT
 DO ZOO.VAL
 STORE 'N' TO MQ:ECMD
 @ 21,10 SAY ' ANY MORE CHANGES (Y/N)? ' GET MQ:ECMD
```

```
     READ
   * PUT SCREEN ENTRIES INTO FILE
     REPLACE ANIMAL WITH MANIMAL
     REPLACE QUANTITY WITH MQUANTITY
     REPLACE DATE WITH MDATE
     REPLACE CAGE:NO WITH MCAGE:NO
     REPLACE SEX WITH MSEX
     REPLACE VALUE WITH MVALUE
     IF !(MQ:ECMD) <> 'Y'
       STORE F TO MQ:EMORE
     ENDIF
   ENDDO
   RELEASE MQ:MODE,MQ:EMORE,MQ:ECMD
     RELEASE MANIMAL
     RELEASE MQUANTITY
     RELEASE MDATE
     RELEASE MCAGE:NO
     RELEASE MSEX
     RELEASE MVALUE
```

The next file is the ZOO.FAU file, used by the ZOO.ADD file.

```
   *     ZOO.FAU      -DEFAULT VALUES PROGRAM
   STORE'                ' TO MANIMAL
   STORE 0 TO MQUANTITY
   STORE '00/00/00' TO MDATE
   STORE 0 TO MCAGE:NO'
   STORE '  ' TO MSEX
   STORE 0 TO MVALUE
```

The following file, ZOO.IO, is used by the ZOO.ADD and ZOO.ED files.

```
   ,*     ZOO.IO-INPUT/OUTPUT SCREEN
     @ 1,0 SAY '--------------------'
```

@ 1,20 SAY '--------------'
@ 1,36 SAY MQ:MODE
@ 1,44 SAY '--------------------'
@ 1,64 SAY '--------------'
@ 2,34 SAY 'ZOO INVENTORY'
@ 4,6 SAY 'ANIMAL'
@ 4,22 GET MANIMAL
@ 5,6 SAY 'QUANTITY'
@ 5,22 GET MQUANTITY PICTURE '999'
@ 6,6 SAY 'DATE'
@ 6,22 GET MDATE PICTURE '99/99/99'
@ 7,6 SAY 'CAGE NUMBER'
@ 7,22 GET MCAGE:NO PICTURE '999'
@ 8,6 SAY 'SEX'
@ 8,22 GET MSEX
@ 9,6 SAY 'VALUE'
@ 9,22 GET MVALUE PICTURE '9999.99'

The next file is the ZOO.OUT file, used by the ZOO.GET file.

```
*    ZOO.OUT    -OUTPUT ONLY FORM
@ 1,0 SAY '--------------------'
@ 1,20 SAY '--------------'
@ 1,36 SAY MQ: MODE
@ 1,44 SAY '--------------------'
@ 1,64 SAY '--------------'
@ 2,34 SAY 'ZOO INVENTORY'
@ 4,6 SAY 'ANIMAL'
@ 4,23 SAY ANIMAL
@ 5,6 SAY 'QUANTITY'
@ 5,23 SAY QUANTITY
@ 6,6 SAY 'DATE'
@ 6,23 SAY DATE
```

```
@ 7,6 SAY 'CAGE NUMBER'
@ 7,23 SAY CAGE:NO
@ 8,6 SAY 'SEX'
@ 8,23 SAY SEX
@ 9,6 SAY 'VALUE'
@ 9,23 SAY VALUE
```

Hang in there; we've almost finished! This is the ZOO.VAL file, used by ZOO.ADD and ZOO.ED.

```
*     ZOO.VAL     -VALIDATION PROGRAM
*VALIDATE MQUANTITY
STORE T TO MQ:VMORE
DO WHILE MQ:VMORE
IF MQUANTITY>= 0
   STORE F TO MQ:VMORE
   ELSE
   @ 23,0 SAY '

   '
   @ 23,0 SAY '  -MUST BE:  >=0'
   @ 5,22 GET MQUANTITY PICTURE '999'
   READ
ENDIF
ENDDO MQUANTITY
VALIDATE MCAGE:NO
STORE T TO MQ:VMORE
DO WHILE MQ:VMORE
IF MCAGE:NO> = 0
   STORE F TO MQ:VMORE
   ELSE
   @ 23,0 SAY '

   '
   @ 23,0 SAY ' - MUST BE: >=0'
@ 7,22 GET MCAGE:NO PICTURE '999'
```

```
    READ
ENDIF
ENDDO MCAGE:NO
*VALIDATE MVALUE
STORE T TO MQ:VMORE
DO WHILE MQ:VMORE
IF MVALUE> = 0
  STORE F TO MQ:VMORE
  ELSE
  @ 23,0 SAY '
  '
  @ 23,0 SAY ' -MUST BE: > = 0'
@ 9,22 GET MVALUE PICTURE '9999.99'

    READ
ENDIF
ENDDO MVALUE
RELEASE MQ:VMORE
```

And last, but not least, is the ZOO.GO file used to generate the index file when you need it.

```
*     ZOO.GO–STARTUP & INDEX PGM
*     USE THIS PGM TO START A KEYED DATA FILE
*     OR RE-INDEX AN EXISTING ONE
SET TALK OFF
SELECT PRIMARY
USE ZOO
INDEX ON ANIMAL TO ZOO
```

That's it! Look at these files; you will probably pick up a few hints for your own files. Remember, your files created by Quickcode in this chapter may be different from the ones shown here, depending on how you designed your ZOO screen.

Chapter 11

dGRAPH

dGRAPH is a complex program, and the documentation provided by Fox & Geller with the program is not as clear as it could be. This chapter touches on dGRAPH's capabilities. But if you plan to use this program, I'd advise a lot of experimentation to develop an understanding of how it works.

The dGRAPH menus you will see on the screen are a little different than the illustrations in this chapter. Special symbols have been used to form the borders, dividers, and other elements. However, the text is reproduced correctly, and the illustrations are accurate enough so that you will be able to follow the instructions in the text.

The dGRAPH program by Fox & Geller can produce many types of charts from your data. You can enter the data directly into the dGRAPH program, get the data from one of your program's data files, or use a dBASE database file. In this chapter, we'll use the STOCK.DBF file from our inventory program to draw a chart from dBASE data.

You may have a newer version of dGRAPH than the one described here, so some of your commands might be different. If things don't work as shown, or if your screens don't match the ones presented here, check your manual for more information.

INSTALLATION

First, back up your dGRAPH diskette(s).

The installation procedure varies according to the type of computer you have and the type of printer you are using. Because of the many possibilities, it's best to use the dGRAPH manual to assist in your installation. Be sure to read any addenda sheets that came with your dGRAPH package before doing the installation.

GRAPHS ON THE SCREEN

The IBM version (and perhaps others) permits you to draw a graph on the monitor screen, instead of, or in addition to, sending the graph to the printer.

To draw a graph on the screen, you *must* have the color/graphics board in your IBM, and the monitor must be connected to this board. If not, you will not be able to display a graph; in fact, the system may give no response, in which case you will have to press the Escape key to regain control of the program. This information does not seem to appear anywhere in the manual. Perhaps the author thought it was too obvious to mention.

THE MAIN MENU

When you start dGRAPH, you will see the main menu screen (Fig. 11-1). You can always work your way back to this screen by using the Escape key from wherever

```
                         dGRAPH Version 1.3
                            Main Menu
IMMMMMMMMMMMMMMMMMMMMMMMMMMMMMMMMMMMMKMMMMMMMMMMMMMMMMMMMMMMMMMMMMMMMMMMM;
:        Start/Set Up dGRAPH             :         Define a Chart         :
:        DDDDDDDDDDDDDDDDDDDD            :         DDDDDDDDDDDDDDD         :
:     T Today's Date    (         )  :   C Chart Name ( NONAME      )  :
:     S System Settings                  :   B Bar        L  Line        :
:     H Help                             :   P Pie        I  Piebar      :
:     ESC to Exit                        :   M Multiple                  :
:                                        :                               :
HMMMMMMMMMMMMMMMMMMMMMMMMMMMMMMMMMMMMMJMMMMMMMMMMMMMMMMMMMMMMMMMMMMMMMMMM<
IMMMMMMMMMMMMMMMMMMMMMMMMMMMMMMMMMMMMMKMMMMMMMMMMMMMMMMMMMMMMMMMMMMMMMMMM;
:        Data Entry                      :        Chart Drawing          :
:        DDDDDDDDDD                      :        DDDDDDDDDDDDDD          :
:     F File Name    ( B:STOCK   )  :   D Draw a Chart             :
:     N New                              :   R Retrieve a Picture        :
:     O Old                              :                               :
:     2 dBASE II File ( C:STOCK   )  :                               :
:                                        :                               :
HMMMMMMMMMMMMMMMMMMMMMMMMMMMMMMMMMMMMMJMMMMMMMMMMMMMMMMMMMMMMMMMMMMMMMMMM<
                    Please Enter Command -->
```

Fig. 11-1. The dGRAPH main menu.

you are in the program. Sometimes you have to use Escape several times to work your way back through other screens to reach this one. Pressing Escape in this menu will return you to your disk operating system. It's like using QUIT from dBASE.

In the upper left corner of the main menu screen, you'll see the start-up choices. Type T and enter the date. You have all the room between the colons for your entry. You could put other information here; the program doesn't check to see if you really entered a date.

Next use F to set the filename. This is the name dGRAPH information will be sent to. Since we will be graphing the dBASE STOCK database, we'll call this file STOCK. If the file will be stored on any drive other than drive A, even if it's the default drive, prefix the filename with the drive name — E:STOCK, for example.

Now use 2 to set the dBASE filename to STOCK, again using a drive prefix if necessary. Of course, we used STOCK because that is the dBASE file we will chart.

Don't use C to set the chart name. This is used to select a chart you previously created; it is *not* used to name the chart that is presently being designed. If you use it, the date and other filenames you just entered will be deleted.

BAR CHARTS

Our first attempt at a graph will create a bar chart. Select B from the main menu. You'll then see something like Fig. 11-2.

Watch for the caret (^) mark; this tells you what data dGRAPH is looking for. To move to the next field, use the RETURN key. If you are accepting a default, use the Tab key; the RETURN key will erase what was there. To back up, use the Backspace key.

Now use F to get to the Fields menu (see Fig. 11-3).

The first data required tells dGRAPH how to treat the data to be graphed. Watch the bottom of the screen. You'll see explanations of the data required, and a list of your choices.

We'll choose SUM. Enter SUM, and then press the RETURN key to go to the next field.

The next entry should be a numeric database field. Note that the fields are listed at the bottom of the screen. Let's use ON:HAND.

The next field is used if we want to use a math expression. We will choose *, for multiply. Other possible choices were /, +, and – (divide, add, and subtract).

The next entry should be the field we wish to multiply ON:HAND by. We'll choose COST.

Since that is the only calculation we want, just press RETURN to go to the row position.

The next choice is for ROW. This is the vertical column that will be graphed. The ROWs can be subdivided into COLUMNs.

For ROW, we'll use the COMPUTER field.

```
IMMM ( NONAME        ) MMMMMMMMMMM BAR GRAPH MMMMMMMMMMM  AutoGraph (YES) MM;
:       ( STOCK       )                                                       :
:                               ZDDDDDDDDDD?                                  :
:                               3         3                                   :
:                               3   <1>   CDDDDDDDDDD?                         :
:                               3         3          3                        :
:                               3         3   <2>    CDDDDDDDDDD?             :
:                               3         3          3         3              :
:                               3         3          3   <3>   CDDDDDDDDDD? :
:                               3         3          3         3         3 :
:                               3         3          3         3   <4>   3 :
:                               @DDDDDDDDDD ADDDDDDDDDD ADDDDDDDDDD ADDDDDDDDDDY :
GDDDDDDDDDDDDDD?                                                              :
:  Selections: @DDDDDDDDDDDDDDDDDDDDDDDDDDDDDDDDDDDDDDDDDDDDDDDDDDDDDDDDDDDDDDDDD& :
:                ( )Titles   ( )Shade   ( )Names   ( )Backup   ( )Options    :
:                ( )Fields   ( )Clear   ( )Draw    ( )Print    ( )Limits     :
:  COMMAND: Please Enter Command Letter ( H for Help ) ==>                    :
:                                                                             :
:                                                                             :
:                                                                             :
:                                                                             :
:                                                                             :
HMMMMMMMMMMMMMMMMMMMMMMMMMMMMMMMMMMMMMMMMMMMMMMMMMMMMMMMMMMMMMMMMMMMMMMMMMMMM<
```

Fig. 11-2.   The dGRAPH bar graph menu.

```
IMMM  (              ) MMMMMMMMMMMMMMMMMMMMMMMMMMMMMMMMMMMMM  AutoGraph (   ) MM;
:                               Column => (        ) (      )                 :
:                               ZDDDDDDDDDD?                                  :
:         Calculation           3         3                                   :
:            (SUM )             3   <1>   CDDDDDDDDDD?                         :
: (            ) ( ) (     ) 3         3          3                        :
:         Data Base Field(s)    3         3   <2>    CDDDDDDDDDD?             :
:                               3         3          3         3              :
:                               3         3          3   <3>   CDDDDDDDDDD? :
:                               3         3          3         3         3 :
:                               3         3          3         3   <4>   3 :
:                               @DDDDDDDDDD ADDDDDDDDDD ADDDDDDDDDD ADDDDDDDDDDY :
GDDDDDDDDDDDDDD?                Row => (        ) (        ) (            ) :
:  Fields:      @DDDDDDDDDDDDDDDDDDDDDDDDDDDDDDDDDDDDDDDDDDDDDDDDDDDDDDDDDDDDDD& :
:           Subject Data Field Totaling Method (default is SUM):             :
:       (SUM) add up all data values  (COUNT) take count of data values      :
:     (AVG) take average of data values  (PCT(S or C)) percentage of SUM or COUNT :
:                       Data fields for C:STOCK.DBF                           :
PART:NO     DESCRIPT   ON:HAND    REORDER     PRICE      COST      SUPPLIER
COMPUTER    ON:ORDER
```

Fig. 11-3.   The dGRAPH bar graph menu, ready for entering fields.

The next entry allows us to use all the data in this field, or selected data. If you wish to select only specific data from your ROW field, you can enter LIST, DATE, or RANGE. If you choose to use any data in the field, use ANY, or just press the RETURN key and get ANY as the default. We'll use ANY.

If you had chosen LIST, you would later be asked for the list of acceptable data. In this case the data could be IBM, APPLE, LISA, and so on.

The RANGE choice possibilities are character strings up to 8 characters long, or numeric data, perhaps 1 to 100.

The date choice allows you to select a specific month, day, or year, with a date format of MM/DD/YY.

Next you will be asked for a column choice. In our database, a possibility might be SUPPLIER. However, to keep this simple, we'll skip choosing a column entry, by pressing the RETURN key.

When you press <RETURN> for the last time, you'll leave the field definition screen. If you used LIST with COLUMN or ROW, you'd now have the opportunity to enter your lists, up to 26 entries for each.

The question about forcing uppercase only affects you if you chose LIST or RANGE. The same applies to the question about exact comparisons. When asked about the dBASE records, use 0 for the first record and 0 (for all) for the number of records to process (see Fig. 11-4).

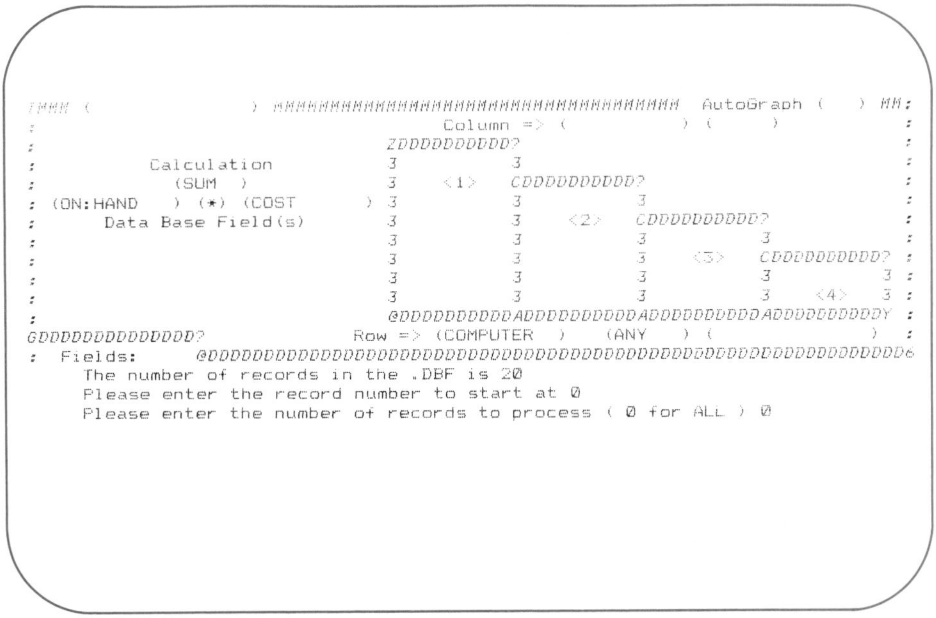

Fig. 11-4. The dGRAPH bar graph menu with fields data entered.

The exceptions report question concerns records whose content does not meet the selection criteria you gave with RANGE, LIST, or DATE.

Note that even if you add or change data in the database, you can still use the chart definition.

If you have a graphics monitor (one plugged into the IBM color/graphics board), go to Options by selecting O (see Fig. 11-5). Set the SCREEN to Y and the PRINT to N. Now your graph will be displayed instead of printed. Printing a graph takes time.

```
IMMM ( NONAME      ) MMMMMMMMMMM BAR GRAPH MMMMMMMMMMM  AutoGraph (YES) MM:
:    ( STOCK       )                                                      :
:   ** Options Mode **          ZDDDDDDDDDD?                              :
:                               3          3                             :
:                               3  <1>   CDDDDDDDDDD?                     :
:                               3          3         3                   :
:                               3          3  <2>  CDDDDDDDDDD?           :
:                               3          3         3         3         :
:                               3          3         3  <3>   CDDDDDDDDDD? :
:                               3          3         3         3        3 :
:                               3          3         3         3  <4>   3 :
:                               @DDDDDDDDDDDADDDDDDDDDDDADDDDDDDDDDDADDDDDDDDDDDY :
GDDDDDDDDDDDDDDD?                                                         :
:  Selections: @DDDDDDDDDDDDDDDDDDDDDDDDDDDDDDDDDDDDDDDDDDDDDDDDDDDDDDDDDD6 :
:                    ( )Titles   ( )Shade   ( )Names   ( )Backup   (X)Options  :
:                    ( )Fields   ( )Clear   ( )Draw    ( )Print    ( )Limits   :
:  COMMAND: Entering Options ( Y-YES, N-NO )                              :
:                                                                         :
:   AutoGraph :Y:   Print   :Y:   Date   :N:      Stack :N:              :
:   Save BTP  :N:   Screen  :N:   Zoom   :N:                             :
:   Save BTS  :N:   Shade   :Y:   Average :N:                            :
:   Text File :N:   Inverse :N:   Accum  :N:                            :
HMMMMMMMMMMMMMMMMMMMMMMMMMMMMMMMMMMMMMMMMMMMMMMMMMMMMMMMMMMMMMMMMMMMMMMMMMM<
```

Fig. 11-5. The dGRAPH bar graph menu, options mode.

If you set both PRINT and SCREEN to Y in the options menu, the graph will first be drawn on the screen, then printed. If you set SCREEN to N and PRINT to Y, the graph will be printed only. You'd use this if you didn't have a color/graphics board.

Now select D for DRAW. The graph will now be drawn on the screen for you. Do you want some titles on it? Use the RETURN key to get back to the bar graph menu and select T.

In Fig. 11-6, SOFTWARE INVENTORY COST was used for the graph title, QUANTITY TIMES COST for the vertical title, and COMPUTER TYPE for the horizontal title. No bar titles were used.

Now select D again to see your graph with titles (see Fig. 11-7).

```
IHHH ( NONAME        ) HHHHHHHHHHHHH BAR GRAPH HHHHHHHHHHHH AutoGraph (YES) HH;
:    ( STOCK        )              Graph Title :SOFTWARE INVENTORY COST  :         :
:   ** Titles Mode **             ZDDDDDDDDDD?                                     :
:                                 3:      :3                                       :
:                                 3   <1>  CDDDDDDDDDD?                             :
:                                 3      3:       :3                               :
:   Vtit :QUANTITY TIMES COST :   3      3   <2>   CDDDDDDDDDD?                     :
:                                 3      3      3:       :3                        :
:                                 3      3      3   <3>   CDDDDDDDDDD? :            :
:                                 3      3      3      3:       :3 :               :
:                                 3      3      3      3   <4>   3 :               :
:                                 @DDDDDDDDDDADDDDDDDDDDADDDDDDDDDDADDDDDDDDDDY :    :
: GDDDDDDDDDDDDDDD?              Htit :COMPUTER TYPE        :                       :
:   Selections: @DDDDDDDDDDDDDDDDDDDDDDDDDDDDDDDDDDDDDDDDDDDDDDDDDDDDDDDDDDDDDDDD6   :
:                  (X)Titles    ( )Shade    ( )Names    ( )Backup   (X)Options     :
:                  ( )Fields    ( )Clear    ( )Draw     ( )Print    ( )Limits      :
:   COMMAND: Entering Vertical Title ( 20 char. max )                             :
:                                                                                 :
:                                                                                 :
:                                                                                 :
:                                                                                 :
HHHHHHHHHHHHHHHHHHHHHHHHHHHHHHHHHHHHHHHHHHHHHHHHHHHHHHHHHHHHHHHHHHHHHHHHHHHHHHHHHH<
```

Fig. 11-6. The dGRAPH bar graph menu with titles entered.

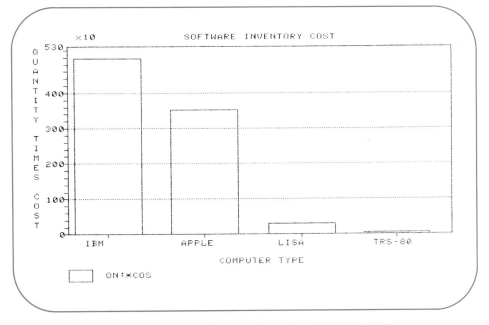

Fig. 11-7. A bar graph created from the STOCK.DBF file.

Note that shading works best if you have more than one column, because only columns show different shading. If you have only one column, as we have, all the columns will be shaded the same. To save printer ribbon and printing time, you might as well leave the shading set to BLANK.

If you select P, you'll print the graph description as follows:

Date — 6/14/84

Graph type — B

File name :

Data file	— E:STOCK
dBase file	— E:STOCK
Text file	— NONAME
Graph save	— E:STOCK

TITLES :

MAIN	— SOFTWARE INVENTORY COST
Horizontal	— COMPUTER TYPE
Vertical	— QUANTITY TIMES COST

Limits :

Minimum value —

Maximum value —

Gridline step —

Tics step —

Options:

Shade	— Y	Autograph	— Y
Zoom	— N	Stack bar	— N
Accum	— N	Print date	— Y
Legend	— N	Text file	— N
Average	— N	dBase file	— Y
Save BTS	— N	Row select	— N
Save BTP	— N	Print chart	— Y
Screen	— N		

If you set SAVE BTP in the Options menu to Y, the data needed to print or display the graph will be saved. This results in a much faster generation of the graph (dGRAPH doesn't have to make all those calculations), but it takes up disk space. Use your own judgment. If you set DATE to Y, the date will be included in the graph. Don't set INVERSE to Y unless you like to buy printer ribbons. Leave TEXT set to N unless you plan to include some text to be printed below the graph. You'll have to create the text file and supply dGRAPH with the filename.

PIE CHARTS

After you have designed the bar chart to your satisfaction, try a pie chart.

Most of the discussion concerning the bar chart holds true for the pie chart. You can set the shades or let Autograph select them for you. In this case, we'll select the default.

You can't use columns in a pie chart, only rows.

We'll use the SUM of ON:HAND * COST again. The chart can be seen in Fig. 11-8.

Pie charts allow only one title, placed horizontally. If you enter a vertical title, it will be displayed horizontally, and any horizontal title you enter will not be used.

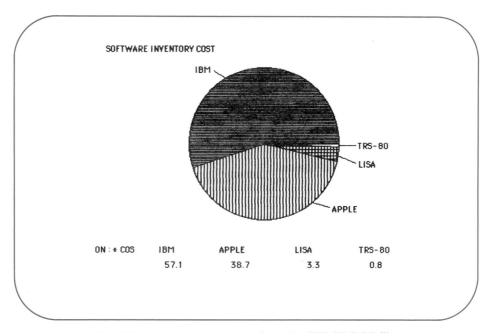

Fig. 11-8. A pie graph created from the STOCK.DBF file.

OTHER GRAPH TYPES

You can also use dGRAPH to generate a line graph or a piebar graph. Try one to see what they are like. The designing process is the same as for the bar chart.

OTHER dGRAPH FEATURES

You can create stacked bar graphs and other combinations.

As mentioned earlier, you can also use dGRAPH to create charts from data you enter directly into the program, or use data created by some other program (perhaps BASIC) and stored in a file. The dGRAPH manual gives a sample BASIC program if you'd like to try this.

Take the time to read the dGRAPH manual to see all the possibilities that exist. The dGRAPH features were only touched on in this chapter. However, you should have learned enough to create simple graphs from your dBASE database files; that may be all you require from dGRAPH.

Chapter 12

_____dBASE II – In Conclusion_____

This chapter will include some odds and ends about dBASE II that haven't been mentioned so far.

_____ABBREVIATIONS_____

All dBASE II commands and key words can be abbreviated to the first four (or more) letters. Thus any of these forms

. disp

. displ

. displa

. display

will work for DISPLAY. Abbreviations were not discussed in the earlier chapters; they can be confusing. Also, the complete word is usually easier to remember and associate with the correct activity than is the abbreviation.

_____NON-dBASE II FILES_____

You can copy a database file to another file, to be used by some other program. Normally, character strings will be delimited with single quotes, and commas will be inserted between the fields. Each group of database fields will be concluded with a carriage return and line feed character. This is standard for CP/M ASCII text files. The statements

. copy to datafile sdf

. copy to datafile.txt sdf

. copy to datafile.txt delimited with '

are all equivalent because the default file type is .TXT and the fault string delimiter is the '. To delimit the strings with double quotes, use

. copy to datafile.txt delimited with "

To generate a file without delimited strings, using only commas between the fields, use

. copy to datafile.txt delimited with ,

Any trailing blanks in the character strings are removed.

To move data from another program's file to dBASE II, the command is

. append from datafile.txt sdf

The dBASE II program assumes the files will have the fields delimited with either single or double quotes, that they will have commas between the fields, and that each group of fields will be concluded with a carriage return line feed sequence.

Of course, the name DATAFILE can be any legal filename. The file-type suffix .TXT will be created by the COPY command unless you override it with another suffix. The suffix for the APPEND command should be indicated in the command.

Obviously, the data being APPENDed must match dBASE II's file structure.

The file transfer schemes described can be used with WordStar and some other word processors — to produce form letters that use mailing lists, for example. The list of names and addresses could be generated by dBASE II.

Some of the spreadsheet programs are designed to work with dBASE II. As an example, let's use SuperCalc. We can transfer the data from SuperCalc in two ways. The spreadsheet data we'll transfer to a dBASE II file is shown in Fig. 12-1.

Here's one good transfer method. First delete the borders from the SuperCalc display with

/GB

Then use the output command to generate an ASCII file.

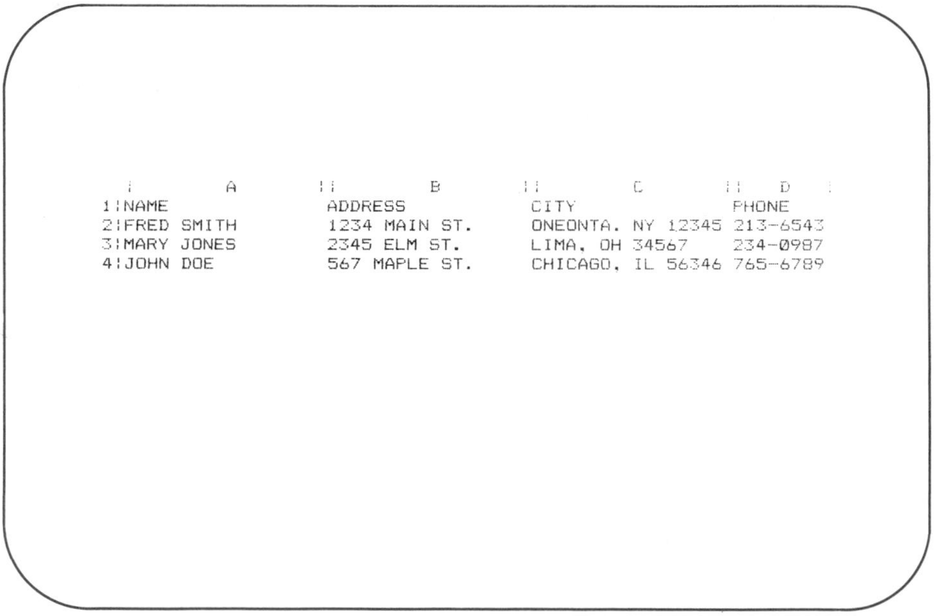

```
     |       A        | |        B         | |        C        | |   D    |
  1 | NAME           | ADDRESS          | CITY            | PHONE    |
  2 | FRED SMITH     | 1234 MAIN ST.    | ONEONTA, NY 12345 213-6543
  3 | MARY JONES     | 2345 ELM ST.     | LIMA, OH 34567   234-0987
  4 | JOHN DOE       | 567 MAPLE ST.    | CHICAGO, IL 56346 765-6789
```

Fig. 12-1. A SuperCalc screen showing spreadsheet data to be transferred.

/Output,Display,A2:D4,Disk,MAILLIST,

Note that the range, (A2:D4), was used to get rid of the titles along the top of the spreadsheet. We now have an ASCII file with the contents of the spreadsheet but without the borders and the top row. Fig. 12-2 shows a printout of the file.

Next we'll APPEND the SuperCalc file to a dBASE II file. First we CREATE the receiving file. To match to the spreadsheet, we must use the same field types (character or numeric) and size.

NAME,C,18

ADDRESS,C,18

CITY,C,18

PHONE,C,8

We named the dBASE II file TESTCALC, so we next

. use testcalc

. append from maillist.prn sdf

```
C>TYPE SUPERCAL\MAILLIST.PRN
FRED SMITH          1234 MAIN ST.       ONEONTA, NY 12345 213-6543
MARY JONES          2345 ELM ST.        LIMA, OH 34567     234-0987
JOHN DOE            567 MAPLE ST.       CHICAGO, IL 56346 765-6789

C>
```

Fig. 12-2.   A SuperCalc-generated .PRN file.

00003 RECORDS APPENDED

. list

00001 FRED SMITH   1234 MAIN ST.   ONEONTA, NY 12345   123-6543

00002 MARY JONES 2345 ELM ST.   LIMA, OH 34567   234-0987

00003 JOHN DOE   567 MAPLE ST. CHICAGO, IL 56346   765-6789

This seems to be the easiest way.

The SuperCalc program has a utility to convert one of its data files to a delimited format (data in quotes with commas between fields), called SDI. But if you use this utility, you get the column heads whether you want them or not.

First create the spreadsheet file as shown in Fig. 12-1 and save it. Now use the SDI program to convert the spreadsheet file to a comma-separated value file, selection A in the SDI menu. We'll use the same name, MAILLIST. The resulting file can be seen in Fig. 12-3.

Next we'll create a dBASE II file, using the same names, types, and sizes as we did for the previous file. Or if you tried the previous method, just use DELETE ALL and PACK to clear the file. The APPEND command for this type of file would be

. append from maillist.csv delimited

```
C>TYPE SUPERCAL\MAILLIST.CSV
"NAME","ADDRESS","CITY","PHONE"
"FRED SMITH","1234 MAIN ST.","ONEONTA, NY 12345","213-6543"
"MARY JONES","2345 ELM ST.","LIMA, OH 34567","234-0987"
"JOHN DOE","567 MAPLE ST.","CHICAGO, IL 56346","765-6789"

C>
```

Fig. 12-3.   A SuperCalc SDI-generated delimited file.

00004 RECORDS APPENDED

. list

00001	NAME	ADDRESS	CITY	PHONE
00002	FRED SMITH	1234 MAIN ST.	ONEONTA, NY 12345	123-6543
00003	MARY JONES	2345 ELM ST.	LIMA, OH 34567	234-0987
00004	JOHN DOE	567 MAPLE ST.	CHICAGO, IL 56346	765-6789

As you can see, the column names from the spreadsheet were also transferred. This could cause a problem if dBASE II was expecting numeric data in that field. An easy way to solve this problem is to use a word processor to get rid of the first record, the one containing the column names.

MAILING LABELS AND CHECKS

With proper formatting, using @ SAY commands, you can use dBASE II to print mailing labels or checks from a database file. This is even easier when Quickcode is used.

THE SED SCREEN EDITOR

A screen editor program (SED) is supplied for the IBM PC version of dBASE II. The 8-bit CP/M version of a similar program is called ZIP.

The screen editor helps you produce a screen format for data entry and display. It is something like Quickcode's Quickscreen feature but it does not create the file structure.

SED is used to arrange the prompts and data entry or display fields on the screen. It relieves you of having to figure out all the correct row and column numbers for your @ SAY and @ GET commands. As in Quickscreen, you enter your prompts using a full-screen editor and indicate the position where the data is to be entered by typing the field variable name that will receive the input at that point.

Instead of using a semicolon, SED uses a <. This means GET the input into the variable following the <.

If you use these simple procedures to set up your screen, SED will write a file with all the @ SAYs and @ GETs for you. If you don't have Quickcode, or don't choose to use it for a particular program, SED will be a big help.

Unlike Quickcode, SED also permits you to add PICTURE clauses to your data variable names, so you can restrict the data entered into them. To use this feature, you enter the PICTURE clause following the variable name.

Because SED uses a previously CREATEd database structure, you don't use suffixes such as $, #, and so on, as you did with Quickcode.

As mentioned earlier, you can use SED to display or print data. This is useful for reports on the screen or printer or for printing mailing labels, checks, forms, and so on. To use this feature, prefix the variable name to be displayed or printed with a >, and position it on the screen where you wish it to be displayed or printed. The screen editor can also be used to display data on the screen in inverse or intensified characters.

SED comes free with dBASE II, so the price is right. It's worth taking the time to learn how to use it, especially if you don't have Quickcode. The editor comes with an excellent on-line help feature that is very detailed. In fact, this is your sole source of documentation, as no manual is provided.

WORD PROCESSORS AND dBASE II

Besides being able to create files that can be used by word processors, and vice versa, you can probably use your word processor to write command files. Try a short command file and see what happens. For example,

```
erase
@ 12,10 say 'it works!'
return
```

It's generally more convenient to use dBASE II's built-in editor to write command files, because it's more trouble than it's worth to QUIT dBASE II and enter a word processing program, just to create a command file. Remember, to write the file DATAFILE.PRG, use

. modify command datafile

Textra Jr. and Microsoft's Word, among others, can be used to create command files. If you're using one of these two processors, you might need to make a few changes in dBASE II. It may be that when you try to DO the word-processor-created file, nothing will happen. Ashton-Tate has supplied the following patch to make dBASE II work with Textra Jr. and Word. This patch is for the IBM version of dBASE II and Textra Jr. or Word. If you have a different version of dBASE II or different word processors, the patch may or may not work.

If you do have the same version of dBASE II and are experiencing the problems described, try this patch on a *copy* of your dBASE II program. It's worth a try. Just make the changes, and then retry your word-processor-created command file to see if it works.

Ashton-Tate Patch for dBASE II

User input is in italics. The <S> is the space bar. The <RETURN> is the carriage return key.

```
>A DEBUG DBASE.COM <RETURN>
−E5662 <RETURN>
1028:5662 0A.E9 <S> CO.3D <S> 75.21 <RETURN>
−E77A2 <RETURN>
1028:77A2 00.3C <S> 00.03 <S> 00.74 <S> 00.04 <S>
         00.08 <S> 00.C0 <S>
1028:77A8 00.75 <S> 00.03 <S> 00.E9 <S> 00.B9 <S>
         00.DE <S> 00.E9 <S>
1028:77AE 00.D4 <S> 00.DE <RETURN>
−W <RETURN>
Writing 7E00 bytes
−Q <RETURN>
>A
```

The DEBUG program is on your DOS Supplement diskette. The dashes are the DEBUG prompts; the >A is the DOS prompt. This assumes your DOS default drive is drive A, DEBUG is in drive A, and the DBASE.COM file is in drive A.

Let's say you have set B as your default drive. Your prompt would then be

>B

Type in A:. You should see

>A

Now put your DEBUG diskette in drive A. Let's say your dBASE II diskette is in drive B. Enter

A> debug b:dbase.com <return>

Now follow the rest of the earlier procedure. Be sure you do your experimenting on a *copy* of DBASE.COM, so that you can always revert to the original if you need to.

Chapter 13

Introducing dBASE III

As this book was being written, Ashton-Tate came out with a new version of dBASE II, called, appropriately enough, dBASE III. This new program is designed to be used with 16-bit microcomputers. The version for the IBM PC, XT, and compatibles is, in most respects, upwardly compatible with dBASE II; that is, most dBASE II commands will work, and several new commands have been added. A major change is that this version is protected. That means that you can't freely generate working copies of the program, as you could with dBASE II. You must have the master diskette, or the backup copy provided by Ashton-Tate, in drive A, or the program will not run. You can transfer all the files to another drive, a hard disk for example, but the master diskette must still be in drive A when the program is started. This protects Ashton-Tate from unauthorized duplication of dBASE III for trade or for sale. You can give a friend a copy of dBASE III, but unless he or she has your master diskette, it can't be run.

The dBASE III program is said to be faster than dBASE II. The tutorial provided with the program documentation is better; it includes a large, annotated sample program. With dBASE III, you can put many more fields in a record and many more records in a file. These are welcome additions. There is a very helpful command called ASSIST that will be very useful to the novice dBASE user. New menu screens are provided for many of the commands, for example, EDIT and APPEND. These menus are helpful when you're learning to use the program. Later on, they can be turned off, if you wish. The system editor has been improved. The REPORT command is easier to use and includes a menu. Now you can edit an existing report form instead of having to redo it completely.

The rest of this chapter will describe changes to commands and features that already exist in dBASE II. The next chapter will describe some of the new dBASE III commands and features.

SYSTEM SPECIFICATIONS

The specifications for dBASE III should not be too hard to meet.

* An IBM Personal Computer, XT, or 100 percent IBM PC-compatible computer
* Minimum 256K bytes RAM memory
* Two 5-¼ inch 360K bytes minimum capacity diskette drives or 1 fixed disk drive and 1 diskette drive
* A monochrome or color display
* The PC-DOS 2.0 operating system
* Any printer with at least 80 columns

The only problem might be for those who have the old single-sided diskette drives or for those who have less than 256K bytes of RAM. Each 64K of RAM costs about $90 from IBM, in addition to the cost of a card required to plug it in. The newer IBM PCs, and all the XTs, have room on the motherboard for 256K bytes of RAM. If you have to add memory for dBASE III, you'll find it quite useful for other programs as well. Most of the newer programs require at least 256K; some require more.

PROGRAM SPECIFICATIONS

Here is a list of the specifications for dBASE III by category.

Each Database File

Number of records	1 billion (maximum)
Number of bytes	2 billion (maximum)
Record size	4,000 bytes in .DBF file
	512K bytes in .DBT file
Fields	128 (maximum)

Field Sizes

Character fields	254 bytes (maximum)
Date fields	8 bytes (maximum)
Logical fields	1 byte (maximum)

| Memo fields | 4096 bytes (maximum) |
| Numeric fields | 19 bytes (maximum) |

File Operations

15 open files of all types

10 open database files; a database file counts
 as two files if memo fields are used.

7 open index files per active database file

1 open format file per active database file

Numeric Accuracy

15 digits; note that the decimal point does
 not count as a digit for determining accuracy.

Largest number: $1 \times 10^{+308}$

Smallest positive number: 1×10^{-307}

Memory Variables

Number of active memory variables: 256

Total bytes for memory variables: 6000

CHANGES TO dBASE II COMMANDS

Memory and Variables

Record field names and memory variable names in dBASE II allowed colons as part of the name. In dBASE III this is not permitted, but you can now use an underline character instead. Thus field and memory variable names can consist of up to 10 letters, digits, or underlines. The first character cannot be an underline character.

The old ERASE command has been changed to CLEAR. Like ERASE, CLEAR is used to clear the screen, and to clear all GETs not yet executed.

CLEAR ALL is used instead of the old CLEAR to close all the files and release all the memory variables. CLEAR GETS is still used to clear pending GETs without erasing the screen. In dBASE III, 128 pending GETs can be used before a CLEAR is required. The dBASE II program allowed only 64 pending GETs.

In addition to RELEASE ALL, another command, CLEAR MEMORY, will also release all the memory variables. In dBASE III, 256 memory variables in 6000 bytes are allowed, instead of 64 in 1536.

Speaking of memory variables, you now have two choices when storing data to a variable. The old

. store 15 to a

is still allowed; however, the more natural

. a = 15

can also be used. This is more like the assignment statement found in most of the higher programming languages.

The accuracy of a numeric variable has been increased from 10 digits to 15 digits.

When you changed a memory variable's type in dBASE II, sometimes the change caused problems. For example,

. store '2' to test
2

. store val(test) to test
    0

As you can see, you couldn't store a variable of changed type to itself. You can do this in dBASE III.

. store '2' to test
2

. store val(test) to test
    2

Logical statements have been changed slightly. Instead of

. store T to test
.T.

? test
.T.

you must use

. store .T. to test
.T.

. ? test
.T.

Also change

> do while T

to

> do while .T.

Files

To see the database filenames available on a diskette, instead of DISPLAY FILES, you now use DIR. You can still pick a drive other than the default and you can still use wildcards. For example,

> . dir b: *.ndx

will show you all the index files on drive B.

To get rid of a file, instead of DELETE FILE, use ERASE. Thus

> . erase test.ndx

will get rid of the TEST index file.

When you are using LIST and DISPLAY, as well as BROWSE, the field names are displayed at the tops of the columns. Also, the complete field names are now shown; they are not truncated to the field width as they were in dBASE II.

When you set up a new index for a file in dBASE II, you had to use

> . use test

> . index on cost to value

> . use test index value

Now you only need

> . use test

> . index on cost to value

The newly created index file is automatically used with the file it was generated from. The second USE command is no longer required. You can still include it if you wish, but it will slow things down.

The dBASE III program documentation no longer warns against using multiple index files when APPENDing, PACKing, and EDITing records. Evidently, the faster program operation has made the use of multiple index files more practical.

The dBASE III program provides a warning if you attempt to COPY or SORT to an existing file. This might save some accidental file erasures.

When SORTing, COPYing, and so on, the records are placed on the screen as the activity proceeds; thus you can watch the command in action.

In dBASE II you could use two database files in a program. They were called PRIMARY and SECONDARY. Now you can use up to 10 files in a program. Instead of PRIMARY, use SELECT 1, instead of SECONDARY, use SELECT 2, and so on, up to SELECT 10. See "ALIAS" in Chapter 14 for more details. Also refer to the "Program Specifications" section earlier in this chapter for additional information.

When FIND fails to locate a record, the record number is set to the last record and EOF( ) is set to TRUE. It used to be that the record number was set to 0 in that case. This change will require modifications to your programs. Following a FIND command, instead of using

    if # = 0

use

    if eof( )

And

    if # <> 0

should be changed to

    if .not. eof( )

Note that EOF has been changed to EOF( ).

In dBASE III the # has been changed to RECNO( ). Thus the old

    . use test
    . ? #
        1

is now

    . use test
    . ? recno( )
        1

Also, * has been changed to DELETION( ). Thus

. delete

. ? *

.T.

is now

. delete

. ? deletion( )

.T.

SORT now works on multiple fields. Thus you can say

. sort on name, address to temp

In dBASE III, MODIFY STRUCTURE can be used on a file without copying it. In dBASE II, when you used MODIFY STRUCTURE, the records were erased. This is no longer true — exactly.

. use test

. list structure

Structure for database   C:TEST.DBF

Number of data records   2

Date of last update   07/30/84

Field	Field name	Type	Width	Dec
1	NAME	C	12	
TOTAL			13	

. list

RECORD#	NAME
1	JOHN
2	MARY

. modify structure

(Use down arrow command to add new field, then ˆEnd)

. list structure

Structure for database   C:TEST.DBF

Number of data records   2

Date of last update   07/30/84

Field	Field name	Type	Width	Dec
1	NAME	C	12	
2	AGE	N	3	
TOTAL			16	

. list

RECORD#	NAME	AGE
1	JOHN	
2	MARY	

When MODIFY STRUCTURE is used, the .DBF file is automatically copied to a .BAK file. When the structure change is complete, the .BAK file is automatically APPENDed to the original .DBF file, with its new structure. A menu is provided to help you with MODIFY STRUCTURE. You should erase the .BAK file when you have finished.

Macros

You can no longer use & macros in a loop. This change was made to increase the program speed. Instead, store the macro result in a variable outside the loop, or use TRIM( ) or something similar.

Utility Programs

The name of the SED program has been changed to dFORMAT. The dFORMAT version has on-line documentation, as did SED. Unfortunately, you must have over 256K bytes of RAM to run this program.

Fox & Geller has come out with new versions of Quickcode and dGRAPH to be used with dBASE III.

Functions

The function for converting to uppercase has been changed from !( ) to UPPER( ). The substring function, $( ) has been changed to SUBSTR( ). (You can still use the $ as an operator in LIST, etc.) The RANK( ) function has been changed to the more natural ASC( ). The substring search function has been changed from @( ) to AT( ).

The "-" concatenate operator has been eliminated. Use the TRIM( ) function instead.

Editing

The full-screen editing commands have been somewhat changed for the better. Remember, the "^" means that you hold down the control (Ctrl) key while pressing the following key. Where more than one key is listed, any of them will work. The Up arrow, Down arrow, Left arrow, Right arrow, Home, End, PgUp, and PgDn keys are those on the keypad. The Ins and Del keys are found under the keypad.

Function	Key(s) to use
Moves cursor back one line or field.	Up arrow, ^E
Moves cursor down one line or field.	Down arrow, ^X
Moves cursor one space left. In menus, moves one choice left.	Left arrow, ^S
Moves cursor one space right. In menus, moves one choice right.	Right arrow, ^D

Moves one field to the right in BROWSE.
   In MODIFY REPORT, it scrolls up.
   In MODIFY COMMAND, it moves the cursor to the end of the line.
	^Right arrow, ^B

Moves one field to the left in BROWSE.
   In MODIFY REPORT, it scrolls down.
   In MODIFY COMMAND, it moves the cursor to the beginning of the line.
	^Left arrow, ^Z

Erases the character to the left of the cursor.	Back arrow (above RETURN)
Erases the character under the cursor.	Del, ^G
Moves the cursor one word right.	End, ^F
Save and exit for full-screen operations.	^End, ^W
Exit without save.	Esc, ^Q
Moves cursor one word left.	Home, ^A
Toggles menus on and off.	^Home

Toggles Insert mode on and off.	Ins, ^V
In MODIFY COMMAND, writes the file to another file.	^KW
In MODIFY COMMAND, reads another file into the file.	^KR
Inserts new line or field definition.	^N
Moves back to previous record or screen display.	PgUp, ^R
Zooms out. (Saves edited text and exits full-screen editor.)	^PgUp, ^W
Moves to next record or screen display.	PgDn, ^C
Zooms in. (Enters full-screen editor and edits memo fields.)	^PgDn
Erases one word right.	^T
Marks record for deletion. Deletes field definition in MODIFY REPORT or MODIFY STRUCTURE.	^U
Erases to end of field, or end of line in MODIFY COMMAND.	^Y
Erases command line.	^X
Stops and starts scroll on screen.	^S

As you can see, most of the old editing commands still work, and alternate keys have been provided. Some useful new commands have been added.

Keyboard Input

The program no longer adds a colon to the prompts following ACCEPT and INPUT. You may wish to add a question mark to the ends of your prompts.

In dBASE II if you pressed the RETURN key in response to an ACCEPT or WAIT statement, a space would be stored to the memory variable, if any, thus:

```
accept to choice
if choice = " "
  . . .
endif
```

This is no longer true. Now a RETURN key response gives a null. So you must use

```
accept to choice
if len(choice) = 0
```

. . .

endif

You can now use a prompt with the WAIT command.

wait "Press any key"

or

wait "Press key to match your choice " to mkey

If the Esc key is used during a dBASE III program, you are not returned to the dot prompt as you were in dBASE II. Instead, you are asked if you wish to stop the program. This could permit a temporary halt in the program.

You can no longer enter a direct command while using STEP in a program.

The method of programming the function keys has been changed. Instead of

set F1 to 'do test;'

use

set function 1 to 'do test;'

Display

The @ SAY USING statement has been changed to @ SAY PICTURE. This command is now consistent with GET.

Long Command Lines

When writing dBASE III programs, you can now use a semicolon (;) at the end of a line to continue on the following line. This makes the code neater than dropping to the next line when the first line fills up. Use it to divide a long line into logical sections. The total line length is still restricted to 254 characters.

Chapter 14

_____More dBASE III_____

This chapter covers the new features in dBASE III that constitute more than changes to dBASE II.

_____CONFIG.DB_____

If you put a file named CONFIG.DB on your start-up diskette, dBASE III will read this file before it provides you with the dot prompt. You can use this feature to SET any program feature; for example, SET CONFIRM OFF. You can also use it to start a program automatically; for example, DO PROGRAM. Then the operator can start the program merely by typing dBASE. You could use a DOS AUTOEXEC.BAT batch file to provide this, so the user would need only to put the disks in the drives and turn on the computer.

_____ASSIST_____

The ASSIST command was mentioned in Chapter 13. It provides a lot of help for the novice user. All you need to do is type ASSIST to the dot prompt and follow the menus to CREATE a file, USE a file, add records, and so on. It would take at least a chapter to describe this feature in detail. As an alternative, just type

. clear all

. assist

and do some experimenting. You'll soon catch on.

DATE AND MEMO

Two new data types have been added to the old character, logical, and numeric types. The new types are memo and date. The *memo* type permits you to store up to 4096 characters in a field. These memo entries are stored in a separate file but can be accessed from the .DBF file as if they were regular fields. When you enter information in this type of field, the program puts you into the word processor. This gives you word wrap and full-screen editing. Just follow the menu.

The *date* type stores the date as a Julian date, which consists of the number of days from 01/01/01 to the given date. This easily allows the program to calculate the day of the week, number of days between two dates, and so on. Many new functions have been provided to use with this new data type. Incidentally, you don't need to know anything about Julian dates to use this feature. You still enter the date as MM/DD/YY.

When a date is entered as input from the keyboard with GET, EDIT, APPEND, or whatever, it is checked to be sure it is valid. Thus you can't enter 01/32/84, 02/30/84, or 13/02/84, for example.

AVERAGE

Besides SUM, TOTAL, and COUNT, you now have an AVERAGE command. An example of its use would be

. average price, cost for cost > 1 to mprice, mcost

where PRICE and COST are record field variables and MPRICE and MCOST are memory variables. This is very similar to the SUM command. The FOR and TO parts are optional.

@ SAY, GET

When you are using @ SAY you have several new features. The $ is no longer used to represent the previous row and column number. You must use ROW( ) or COL( ) instead. To erase the screen to the right and below a set of coordinates, use @ X,Y CLEAR where X is the row number and Y is the column number.

A number of additions have been made to the PICTURE clause. All the old characters still work. The new ones are as follows:

Functions

C   Displays CR (credit) after a positive number.

X   Displays DB (debit) after a negative number.

(Encloses negative numbers in parentheses.

B   Left justifies numeric data.

Z   Displays zero numeric value as a blank string.

D   American date format (MM/DD/YY).

E   European date format (DD/MM/YY).

R   Literals in the template; not considered to be part of the data.

Template symbols

L   Allows logical data

N   Allows letters and digits

These symbols are in addition to those described for dBASE II. When using a function in a PICTURE clause, preface it with an @. For example,

@ 0,0 clear

@ 10,15 say 'A' get mdate picture '@D'

@ 11,25 say mvalue picture '@(CX ##,###.##'

The GET statement may now be followed by an optional RANGE clause. This sets the minimum and maximum limits of numeric or date entries, thus:

@ 10,10 say 'value ' get mvalue range 1,99

or

@ 10,10 say 'date ' get mdate range 01/01/83,12/31/83

The program will respond with an error message until the READ value falls in the specified range.

ALIAS

Chapter 13 mentioned that you can have up to 10 database files open at one time. To do so you use the statements SELECT 1, SELECT 2, and so on. As you open the file in each new area (1 to 10) with USE, each file is automatically given an ALIAS. The file opened in area 1 is given an ALIAS of A, the one in area 2 an ALIAS of B, and so on. These As, Bs, and other characters are used almost like the P and S were used for PRIMARY and SECONDARY with dBASE II. Here's a quick example.

```
select 1
use first
select 2
use second
if a->hours > 40 then store .T. to ot
. . .
```

In this case, the A->HOURS means that if the HOURS field in the record in database FIRST is greater than 40, then OT is set to TRUE. You can also assign an alias of your choice to a file, thus:

```
. use personnl alias salary
```

or

```
. use personnl index name, dept alias salary
```

REPORTS

You can use CREATE REPORT to fill out a report form. This is done with the aid of a menu, so it is quite simple. Also, now you can have several (up to four) headings for a column, and the same number of expressions displayed under the headings. This means you are no longer tied to the width of the paper for your printed headings and data. Also, the program keeps track of how much remains of the report width you have chosen (or defaulted to). Just follow the menu.

You also have a MODIFY REPORT command, so you can change a report without reentering the whole thing as you had to do in dBASE II.

PUBLIC AND PRIVATE VARIABLES

The PUBLIC statement is used to declare variables as global. Any program can use them. They are not released when a program terminates. A variable must not be initialized (given any value) before being declared PUBLIC.

. public name, address, zip

The PRIVATE statement hides any higher-level definition of the declared variables from the current subroutine and any lower-level subroutine that's called. A variable in a subroutine designated PRIVATE can have (usually has) the same name as a previously used variable. The subroutine's variables are released (their data is lost) when the subroutine RETURNs to a higher-level program.

. private mprice, mcost

CLOSE

The CLOSE command can be used to close open files of all sorts. The permitted arguments following CLOSE are

ALTERNATE

DATABASES

FORMAT

INDEX

PROCEDURE

For example,

. close index

closes all open index (.NDX) files. And

. close databases

closes all open database (.DBF) files. Only one argument is permitted for each CLOSE. Thus,

. close index, databases

is *not* allowed.

COPYING

You can quickly copy any file to another filename with

. copy file test.dbf to temp.dbf

In this case, when a database file is copied, if there are any memo fields, the file with memo fields must be copied separately.

. copy file test.dbt to temp.dbt

You can copy files other than database files. For example,

. copy file test.ndx to temp.ndx

or

. copy file test.prg to temp.prg

The file being copied from or to cannot be open. Notice that the file extension must be included.

The COPY STRUCTURE command is used to copy an open .DBF file's structure (no records included) to another file. For example,

. use test

. copy structure to temp

An optional field list can be included:

. copy structure to temp fields name, address, zip

LABEL COMMANDS

The CREATE LABEL and MODIFY LABEL commands work the same way. These commands are used to create or edit a label format file for the active database. Just follow the menu instructions. CREATE LABEL and MODIFY LABEL make it convenient to produce mailing labels from a name and address database file.

The LABEL FORM command does the actual printing. If we assume the label format file has been created and has the filename TEST__LABEL, then to print the labels we use

. label form test__label to print for zip > 12000

As usual, the FOR is optional. There are other options, too. One other is

. label form test__label sample to print

This prints a sample row of labels so you can check the registration.

REMARKS

NOTE is the same as *. It is used at the beginning of a program line to indicate that the line is a remark or comment.

PASSING VARIABLES

The PARAMETERS statement is used to pass values from a program to a called program, thus:

do calculate with cost, price, quantity

. . .

* command file calculate

parameters C, P, Q

* P = price, C = cost, Q = quantity

store (P-C)*Q in mprofit

return

As shown, the program sending the parameters uses a WITH clause in the DO statement to accomplish this.

RUNNING OTHER PROGRAMS FROM dBASE III

You can use the RUN command to run any DOS program from dBASE III without leaving the program; you can run a text editor, for example. Unfortunately, more than 256K bytes of memory are usually required — sometimes quite a few more, depending on the program you run. The RUN command is entered this way:

. run WordStar

SEEK

The SEEK command works a lot like FIND. It searches very quickly for one or more key fields that match the expression following SEEK. If the record is not found, EOF( ) is set to TRUE. If the expression includes a string literal, the string must be enclosed in delimiters. For example, use namefile index f__name

seek 'MARY'

if .not. eof( )

. . .

endif

ZAP

If you wish to remove all the records from a database file quickly, this is the command to use. It is faster than using COPY STRUCTURE, and then COPYing the file back, another way to do the same thing. ZAP works on the selected open file. It checks first to be sure you really want to erase all those records.

NEW SET TO AND SET STATEMENTS

There are several new SET statements in dBASE III.

SET COLOR TO

SET COLOR TO is followed by one or more color codes. The codes are as shown in Table 14-1.

Table 14-1. **dBASE III color codes**

Color	Letter code	Number code
Black	space	0
Blue	B	1
Green	G	2
Cyan	BG	3
Red	R	4
Magenta	BR	5
Yellow	GR	6
White	W	7

The first argument following SET COLOR TO is the standard color and background; the second is for enhanced color and background (optional); and the third is the border color (optional). The colors can be indicated with letter code or number code. Thus

. set color to B/W,R/BG,GR

would set the standard color to blue with white background, enhanced color to red with cyan background, and the border to yellow. The same thing could be accomplished by using number codes:

. set color to 1/7,4/3,6

SET DECIMALS TO

This works with the new SQRT( ), EXP( ), and LOG( ) functions or with a division result. It determines the number of decimal places produced by these commands. The default is two places.

SET DELIMITER

If SET DELIMITER OFF is used, fields in the full-screen mode are shown in reverse video. If the ON setting is used, the fields are delimited with colons. SET DELIMITER TO lets you select the delimiters. One or two characters can be used. If only one character is used, it marks both the beginning and end of the field. If two characters are used, the first character marks the beginning, the second the end. If you use

. set delimiter to '!'

then exclamation points are used to delimit the fields. If you use

. set delimiter to '<>'

then the '<' is used to mark the beginning of the field and the '>' marks the end.
The default for SET DELIMITER is OFF.

SET DEVICE TO

This determines where the @ commands will be sent. The two possible arguments are SCREEN and PRINTER. The default is SCREEN.

SET FILTER TO

FILTER is used to select only specific records. It works the same way as the FOR clause. Thus,

. list for city = 'CHICAGO'

could be replaced with

. set filter to city $ 'CHICAGO'

. list

To turn off the filter use

. set filter to

SET FIXED

SET FIXED ON sets all numeric output to whatever was set in the SET DECIMALS statement. If SET DECIMALS was not used, then the default is two decimal places. If SET FIXED is OFF, the SET DECIMALS affects only the LOG( ), EXP( ), SQRT( ), and division results. The default is OFF.

SET FORMAT TO

You can create a file with a screen description in it — that is, a series of @ SAY GET statements or ? statements that display the screen format desired. To use one of these files, use SET FORMAT TO with that filename. The format file must have an .FMT extension. This display is then used for APPEND, CHANGE, EDIT, INSERT, and so on.

SET MENU

Use SET MENU to turn the menus on and off. They'll be useful at first, but soon you won't need them any more. The default is ON.

SET PATH TO

SET PATH TO works the way the DOS PATH command does. Provide a list of directory paths, separated with commas, following this statement.

SET PROCEDURE TO

When we wrote programs in dBASE II, as in Chapter 8, we kept all the programs small and called them from the disk as we needed them. While this is a convenient way to program, it does take time to load each file from the diskette. In dBASE III, we have what are called *procedures*. After all the small program modules have been checked and debugged, you should combine them into one big file, and then rename each of the original small programs as a PROCEDURE. For example, if one of the program names is REORDER, then you name it PROCEDURE REORDER in the combined file. It will still be called as DO REORDER, so you won't have to change your program. The PROCEDURE names are used only to separate the programs in the combined file. Be sure that each procedure in the combined file ends with a RETURN.

Although DO REORDER will run the REORDER procedure as mentioned earlier, it won't load the file containing the procedure into memory. The combined file must have a name, and it must be loaded separately. To load this file we use SET PROCEDURE TO, followed by the name of the combined file. If the file extension is not .PRG, then it must be included in the filename. A procedure file can contain a maximum of 32 procedures. Only one procedure file can be open at a time. To close a procedure file use CLOSE PROCEDURE.

You don't have to use procedures, but they will speed your program up, especially if it is on floppy disk and uses a lot of short, frequently called programs, as the Quickcode programs do.

SET RELATION TO

This replaces the SET LINKAGE TO in dBASE II. It is used to link two database files together by key data. For best results, the key data should be unique. As a record is selected in the active database, the second database, indexed on a key that occurs in the active database, is searched, and the first record that is found with the matching key is selected. Thus the two files can be synchronized. The second file is designated with its ALIAS. For example,

. set relation to address into filename

where ADDRESS is the key, and FILENAME is the ALIAS of the second file.

SET SAFETY

Remember dBASE III warns you if you attempt to write over an existing file when you COPY or SORT, for example. To defeat this, SET SAFETY OFF. The default is ON.

SET UNIQUE

If you set UNIQUE to ON before you INDEX a file, the index keys will all be unique. Any records with duplicate keys will be ignored in the indexing process. Therefore, some of the records may be skipped when this index is used. Be sure to set UNIQUE to OFF when you have completed the INDEX. If it is left ON and a record is added or changed, the index file may not be updated correctly. The default is OFF.

SET STATEMENTS NOT
FOUND IN dBASE III

The following SET statements from dBASE II are not available in dBASE III.

SET SCREEN

SET LINKAGE

SET COLON

SET EJECT

SET RAW

NEW FUNCTIONS

There are several new functions in dBASE III.

BOF( )

BOF( ) is the opposite of EOF( ). It is set to TRUE if you attempt to move upward past the first record (Beginning Of File).

CDOW( )

If you put a variable containing a date within the parentheses, this function will return the day of the week.

. store cdow(date( )) to dayweek

Tuesday

. ? dayweek

Tuesday

Remember, DATE( ) returns the system date.

CMONTH( )

This function returns the name of the month from a date variable. For example,

. store cmonth(date( )) to month

July

. ? month

July

COL( )

COL( ) was discussed earlier, under @ SAY.

CTOD( )

CTOD( ) converts a date stored in a string to the date type.

. store '07/31/84' to thisdate

07/31/84

. ? type(thisdate)

C

. store ctod(thisdate) to thisdate

07/31/84

. ? type(thisdate)

D

DAY( )

DAY( ) returns the numeric value of the day in a date variable. For example,

. store day(date( )) to thisday

31

. ? thisday

31

DOW( )

DOW( ) gives you the numeric representation of the day of the week, where Sunday is 1. If the system date is 7/31/84 (a Tuesday), then

. ? dow(date( ))

3

EXP( )

EXP( ) is a math function that returns the value of e^x, where e = 2.71828 . . . .

. store 1.000 to X

. ? exp(X)

2.718

LOG( )

Like EXP( ), LOG( ) is a math function. It returns the natural logarithm (to the base e) of a number.

. store 2.71828 to X

. ? log(X)

     1.00000

LOWER( )

LOWER( ) is the opposite of UPPER( ). It converts uppercase characters to lowercase.

. store ABC to test

. ? lower(test)

abc

MONTH( )

If you'll remember, CMONTH returned the name of the month from a date variable. The MONTH function returns the numeric representation of the month. If the system date is 7/31/84, then

. ? month(date( ))

7

PCOL( )

To get the column position of the printhead, type

. ? pcol( )

35

The result indicates that the printer position is presently located at column 35.

PROW( )

PROW( ) is like PCOL( ), but it gives the printer's row location.

ROUND( )

ROUND( ) will round off a numeric value to a specific number of decimal places.

. store 9.123456 to X

. ? round(X,5)

        9.12345

. ? round(X,2)

        9.12

ROW( )

ROW( ) was discussed earlier, under @ SAY GET.

SPACE( )

A character string of spaces is the result of using the SPACE( ) function. For example,

. store space(3) to room

. ? 'XX' + room + 'YY'

XX   YY

SQRT( )

To get the square root of a number, use the SQRT( ) function.

. ? sqrt(9)

        3

. ? sqrt(144)

        12

TIME( )

TIME( ) is similar to DATE( ), but it returns the system time, thus:

. ? time( )

08.26.32

The time format is HH.MM.SS.

YEAR( )

The response to YEAR( ) is the complete numeric representation of the year in a date variable. For example,

. ? year(date( ))

1984

THE FILE CONVERSION PROGRAM

If you have a number of files that you have been using with dBASE II and now wish to start using them with dBASE III, you don't have to start over. The DCONVERT program will convert .DBF, .MEM, .FRM. .PRG, and .NDX files from the dBASE II format to dBASE III format.

DCONVERT is easy to use. Let's say you wish to put your dBASE II files in drive A and store the converted files on drive B. Just enter

dconvert A: B:

If you want both groups of files on one diskette, use

dconvert

The files should then be placed in the drive where the DCONVERT program was located. The diskette receiving the files must have been formatted.

When the conversion is made, the original dBASE II file is not changed, except that the last letter of the file extension is changed to a B. Thus TEST.DBF after conversion would be TEST.DBB. The B stands for backup.

When .PRG files are converted, you will have to check the old and new listings side by side to be sure everything is all right. As you noted in these last two chapters, some things were changed in the development of dBASE III. For example, no macros are allowed in a loop. If you have used macros within a loop, you will have to make the necessary changes to your file manually. Most of the dBASE II program lines will be converted to dBASE III correctly. But be sure to make a line-by-line comparison.

Files other than .PRG files should all convert with no problem. Note that some of the resulting files may be larger, because of the increased numeric accuracy.

The DCONVERT program uses menus and has the HELP aid. Look at the material in the back of the program manual after the index for more information about the changes in dBASE III and using the conversion program.

Index

!, 103, 117, 222
#, 96, 117, 160, 220
$, 49, 87, 97, 117, 153, 160, 163, 222, 228
&, 61, 99
(, 229
*, 100, 117, 220, 233
+, 49
−, 49, 223
−>, 230
9, 117
;, 225
<, 48, 212
=, 48
>, 48, 212
?, 35, 44, 85, 158
@, 85, 102, 153, 222, 229
^A, 223
^B, 32, 159, 223
^C, 158, 224
^D, 157, 223
^E, 157, 223
^END, 223
^F, 158, 223
^G, 158, 223
^HOME, 223
^INS, 224
^J, 158
^KR, 224
^KW, 224
^L, 158

^Left arrow, 223
^N, 224
^O, 158
^P, 158
^PgDn, 224
^PgUp, 224
^Q, 31, 158, 223
^R, 224
^Right arrow, 223
^S, 157, 223, 224
^T, 158, 224
^U, 34, 37, 158, 224
^V, 158, 224
^W, 32, 82, 158, 223, 224
^X, 157, 223, 224
^Y, 68, 158, 224
^Z, 32, 223
^—, 159

A

A, 117
Abbreviations of commands and key words,
   207
ACCEPT, 84, 224
Accuracy, numeric, 14, 217, 218
Addition, 46
ALIAS, 220, 229
ALL, with commands, 34, 35, 45, 66, 67, 68
   77, 78, 116
ALTERNATE, 231
.AND., 48

245

☐ MANAGING WITH dBASE III

A detailed guide to using dBase III in business. A wealth of common business applications can be incorporated into dBase III, such as inventory control, accounts payable and accounts receivable, and business graphics. Michael J. Clifford.
ISBN 0-672-22455-0 . . . . **$19.95**

☐ THE BEST BOOK OF: SYMPHONY

Learn basic and advanced techniques for using Symphony with this excellent introductory tutorial. Provides an in-depth discussion of all of Symphony's features. Includes sample spreadsheets for many common business applications, sample data base for form letters and mailing labels, complete communication examples, and instructions for interfacing Symphony with other popular business software systems. Alan Simpson.
ISBN 0-672-22420-8 . . . . **$21.95**

☐ THE BEST BOOK OF: FRAMEWORK

An introductory tutorial for Framework users. Contains easy hands-on examples, basic and advanced techniques for using Framework to its fullest. Discusses all of Framework's features including sample spreadsheets for many common business applications such as stock portfolio, financial projection, and loan amortization. Includes sample form letters, communications examples with business services, and instructions for interfacing Framework with other business software systems. Alan Simpson.
ISBN 0-672-22421-6 . . . . **$15.95**

☐ THE BEST BOOK OF: LOTUS 1-2-3

Lotus 1-2-3 is a great and wondrous toolbox, waiting for you to open it up. Beginners crack the lid . . . but this book takes the lid off and teaches you to master all the powerful features available in the program. Alan Simpson.
ISBN 0-672-22307-4 . . . . **$12.95**

☐ DISCOVERING KNOWLEDGEMAN™

Dynamic, powerful learning tool that quickly shows you how to use the KnowledgeMan information management system. Introduces its data management and spreadsheet capabilities, and goes on to teach you how to use each feature by actually working with the program in a step-by-step approach. Excellent tutorial. Micro Data Base Systems, Inc.
ISBN 0-672-22415-1 . . . . **$19.95**

☐ THE BEST BOOK OF: MULTIPLAN

Multiplan was designed to be easy to use and it is, but taking full advantage of the hidden powers of the program takes more exploration. Best Book of Multiplan provides tips, tricks, and secrets which will enable you to design more efficient and useful models. Alan Simpson.
ISBN 0-672-22336-8 . . . . **$11.95**

☐ CP/M BIBLE: THE AUTHORITATIVE REFERENCE GUIDE TO CP/M

Already a classic, this highly detailed reference manual puts CP/M's commands and syntax at your fingertips. Instant one-stop access to all CP/M keywords, commands, utilities, and conventions are found in this easy-to-use format. If you use CP/M, you need this book. Waite and Angermeyer.
ISBN 0-672-22015-6 . . . . **$19.95**

☐ CP/M® PRIMER (2nd Edition)

This tutorial companion to the CP/M Bible is highly acclaimed and widely used by novices and advanced programmers alike. Includes the details of CP/M terminology, operation, capabilities, internal structure, plus a convenient tear-out reference card with CP/M commands. This revised edition allows you to begin using new or old CP/M versions immediately in any application. Waite and Murtha.
ISBN 0-672-22170-5 . . . . **$16.95**

☐ SOUL OF CP/M: HOW TO USE THE HIDDEN POWER OF YOUR CP/M SYSTEM

Recommended for those who have read the CP/M Primer or who are otherwise familiar with CP/M's outer layer utilities. This companion volume teaches you how to use and modify CP/M's internal features, including how to modify BIOS and use CP/M system calls in your own programs. Waite and Lafore.
ISBN 0-672-22030-X **$19.95**

☐ C™ PRIMER PLUS

Who better to explain the intricacies of C and UNIX than the master of systems? It's Waite at his best. Provides a clear and complete introduction to the C programming language. This well illustrated primer guides you in the proper use of C programming methodology. Interfacing C with assembly language is included, as well as many sample programs usable with any standard C compiler. Build a sound working knowledge of the language with C Primer Plus. Waite, Prata, and Martin.
ISBN 0-672-22090-3 . . . . **$19.95**

COMPAQ is a registered trademark of COMPAQ Computer Corporation • IBM is a registered trademark of International Business Machines, Inc. • KnowledgeMan is a trademark of Micro Data Systems, Inc. • MemoMaker is a registered trademark of Hewlett-Packard • MS DOS is a trademark of Microsoft Corporation • Panasonic is a registered trademark of Pansonic Industrial Company • PC DOS is a trademark of International Business Machines, Inc. • Sr. Partner is a trademark of Panasonic Industrial Company.

☐ DISCOVERING MS-DOS

The Microsoft generic version of DOS for the IBM PC is given the unique Waite touch. From complete description of the basic command set through analysis of architectural implications, you will gain a complete understanding of this operating environment. Kate O'Day.
ISBN 0-672-22407-0 . . . . **$15.95**

☐ MS-DOS BIBLE

A step beyond DISCOVERING MS-DOS. Take an in-depth look at MS-DOS, particularly at commands such as DEBUG, LINK, EDLIN. Provides quick and easy access to MS-DOS features, clear explanations of DOS utilities, and tutorials which illustrate the concepts presented. Handy pin-up table easily references commands. Steve Simrin.
ISBN 0-672-22408-9 . . . . **$18.95**

☐ MS-DOS DEVELOPER'S GUIDE

If you have a working knowledge of 8088 ALC, this book will help you learn the tips and tricks needed to get your software running in the MS-DOS environment. The book offers assembly coding tips, explains the differences between MS-DOS versions, the MS-DOS bios, and higher-level language debuggers and aids. Angermeyer and Jaeger.
ISBN 0-672-22409-7 . . . . **$21.95**

☐ PRINTER CONNECTIONS BIBLE

At last! A book that teaches non-technical people how to connect a computer to a printer. Covers major computer/printer combinations, supplies detailed diagrams of required cables, dip-switching settings, etc. The book is graphically oriented with diagrams illustrating numerous printer/computer combinations. House and Marble.
ISBN 0-672-22406-2 . . . . **$16.95**

☐ IBM PC/PC*jr* LOGO PROGRAMMING PRIMER

Quickly learn and use the complete Logo language to plan and write useful, fascinating programs that do exactly what you have in mind. Emphasizes structured, top-down programming techniques with box charts that help you discipline yourself for maximum effectiveness in planning, changing, and debugging Logo programs. Covers recursion, outputs, and utilities. Features include clear and concise diagrammatic explanations of Logo syntax. Several sample programming projects included. Martin, Prata, and Paulsen.
ISBN 0-672-22379-1 . . . . **$24.95**

☐ MODEM CONNECTIONS BIBLE

Put what where? This comprehensive volume describes modems and how they work. Detailed diagrams explain how to hook up major brands of microcomputers. Find out what happens with the RS-232C interface. A must for microcomputer users and technicians. Richmond and Majhor.
ISBN 0-672-22446-X **$24.95**

☐ PC DOS™ COMPANION

DOS need no longer be a mystery. This clearly written, abundantly illustrated introduction to PC DOS 1.0, 1.1, and 2.0 for PC and XT™ users covers PC DOS commands and the relationship of DOS to applications software. Tips on the best use for each command and a handy command reference card complete this vital reference book. Murtha and Petrie.
ISBN 0-672-22039-3 . . . . **$15.95**

☐ THE PERFECT GUIDE TO PERFECT WRITER ™

Explains items left unclear in the manufacturer's *Perfect Writer* manual. Strips away confusion and shows you clearly how to use this powerful word processing program. Logical organization, excellent illustrations, and other organizational aids bring the best out of beginners and advanced users. Dona Z. Meilach.
ISBN 0-672-22186-1 . . . . **$17.95**

☐ SUPERCALC PRIMER

A step-by-step format and superb organization make this reference book a must-buy for businessmen and other *SuperCalc* users. Sticky calculations and complex formulas will no longer get in your way. Stop trying to learn *SuperCalc* and start using it with the many practical business examples provided. Waite, Burns, and Venit.
ISBN 0-672-22087-3 . . . . **$16.95**

☐ 8088 ASSEMBLER LANGUAGE PROGRAMMING: THE IBM PC

There is life after BASIC. This book gives you a comprehensive introduction to writing machine-language software for use with the IBM PC. Functionally describes the 8088 microprocessor and furnishes detailed information about the PC's internal structure. Some programming experience required. Willen and Krantz.
ISBN 0-672-22024-5 . . . . **$15.95**